CHILD WELFARE LEAGUE OF AMERICA

STANDARDS FOR SERVICE FOR ABUSED OR NEGLECTED CHILDREN AND THEIR FAMILIES

Child Welfare League of America
Washington, DC

CHILD WELFARE LEAGUE OF AMERICA, INC.
440 First Street, NW, Suite 310, Washington, DC 20001-2085

Current Printing (last digit)
10 9 8 7 6 5 4 3 2 1

PRINTED IN THE UNITED STATES OF AMERICA

ISBN 0-87868-353-4

These standards are dedicated to the memory of two individuals whose lives were devoted to children and their families:

Richard J. Bond began his professional career in 1950 as a group worker at Children's Aid Society, which later became Boston Children's Service Association (BCSA). His career then took him first to Connecticut, where he served as Executive Director of the Connecticut Junior Republic from 1956–1966, then to Ohio to head the Cincinnati Children's Home for four years, and then to Illinois, where he served as director of child welfare services for the state. In 1973 he returned to Massachusetts as Executive Director of BCSA. Mr. Bond was the Chairman of the 1972 CWLA Standards for Child Protective Service Committee.

Robert M. Mulford spent most of his career serving as Executive Director of the Massachusetts Society for the Prevention of Cruelty to Children from 1947 to his retirement in 1979. He served as the CWLA staff consultant in the writing of the 1959 Standards and as a member of the 1972 CWLA Standards for Child Protective Service Committee.

CONTENTS

FOREWORD

Setting standards and improving practice in all child welfare services have been major goals of the Child Welfare League of America since its formation in 1920. With the issuance of these standards, CWLA reaffirms its commitment to establish standards that can be used as goals for practice. As we continue to learn more about the essentials for the healthy growth of children, CWLA can help to redefine the responsibility of society to provide for children the conditions and opportunities that encourage individual growth and development.

Since the inception of its program of standards development, CWLA has formulated a series of standards based on current knowledge, the developmental needs of children, and tested ways of meeting these needs effectively. The preparation of standards involves an examination of current practices and the assumptions on which they are based; a survey of the professional literature and standards developed by others; and a study of the most recent scientific findings of social work and related fields such as child development, education, mental health, psychology, medicine, psychiatry, and sociology, as they bear on child welfare practice.

The final formulation of standards follows an extended discussion of principles and issues by committees of experts in each service, the drafting of a preliminary statement, and a critical review by CWLA member agencies and representatives of related professions and other national organizations.

CWLA's preparation of standards involves the wide participation of local, state, provincial, and national agency representatives. Many CWLA member agencies, including state or provincial human service departments as well as private agencies, have contributed professional time and travel costs of staff members who have reviewed draft statements and made suggestions for revision. National organizations, including governmental agencies, sectarian agencies, and professional associations in related fields, have taken part in the overall planning and the work of the various committees.

The process of setting standards provides an opportunity to reexamine goals, to redefine objectives, to clarify concepts, and to reaffirm convictions about what we want for children and believe society should provide for them.

Purpose of Standards

These standards are intended to be goals for the continuing improvement of services for children. They are not the criteria for CWLA membership, although they are used in the development of the provisions of the Council on Accreditation of Services for Families and Children, Inc. (COA). They represent those practices considered to be most desirable in providing the services that the community offers through its various agencies.

The standards are directed to all who are concerned with the improvement of services to children and their families: the general public, citizen groups, public officials, legislators, and various professional groups; those responsible for the provision of services—board members and agency staff members; agencies whose functions include planning and financing community services; state or provincial agencies entrusted by law with functions relating to the licensing or supervision of organizations serving children; and federations whose membership requirements involve judgments on the nature of services rendered by member agencies.

Standards can stimulate improvement of services only as they generate dissatisfaction with present practices and a conviction that change is desirable. They offer a base to examine and measure practice, the premises from which it has developed, and the performance of child welfare agencies and their current services.

Standards are of use in planning, organizing, and administering services; in establishing state, provincial, and local licensing requirements; and in determining the requirements for accreditation. Standards provide content for teaching and training in child welfare and other related fields, in professional schools, in inservice training and staff development programs, and in the orientation of boards and volunteers. They can help to explain and justify expenditures and budget requests to fundraising bodies, and appropriation requests to legislatures.

Finally, standards can promote understanding of how each service may more effectively meet the needs of children, what it should be expected to do, and how it can be used. In that way, standards can help to gain greater public interest, understanding, and support for providing services, targeting legislation, and improving financing.

Review of Standards

The Child Welfare League of America continues to periodically review all standards at appropriate times. No practice standards should be considered final; in one sense, soon after they are issued they are out of date. Standards must be subject to continual review and revision since knowledge about children, human ehavior, and the treatment of human ills grows constantly. Developments in the ocial and medical sciences; the continuing evaluation of the effectiveness of current social work practices, policies, and programs; and shifting patterns of social values and social organization must lead to change in child welfare practice.

Toward this end, CWLA responded in May of 1987 with the formulation of the CWLA National Child Protective Service Standards Committee. The committee consisted of representatives of member agency providers from both the public and voluntary sectors, representatives from other national organizations, researchers, and other protective service experts. The group's task was to revise the current national standards for this field of child welfare practice.

The committee met several times during 1987 and 1988. A draft was produced with CWLA staff support. The draft was circulated to the CWLA membership and other interested agencies and individuals for review before it was submitted to the CWLA Board of Directors in May 1988 for approval.

It is hoped that these newly revised standards will lead to the improvement and development of new and better services to protect all children and their families.

Mai Bell Hurley
President
Child Welfare League of America, Inc.

David S. Liederman
Executive Director
Child Welfare League of America, Inc.

ACKNOWLEDGMENTS

This edition of the Child Welfare League of America *Standards for Services for Abused or Neglected Children and Their Families* was prepared by a committee whose members were selected on the basis of their expertise in child protective service. The committee represents CWLA member agencies, other national organizations, researchers, and allied professions concerned with abused or neglected children and their families. The committee received, discussed, and incorporated the suggestions made from member agencies—state, provincial, local, public, and voluntary.

The Board of Directors of the Child Welfare League of America approved these *Standards for Services for Abused or Neglected Children and Their Families* on May 19, 1988.

Committee on Standards for Services for Abused or Neglected Children and Their Families

Chair: Peter E. Walsh, Maine Department of Human Services, Augusta, ME

Participants: Thomas L. Birch, National Coalition for the Prevention of Child Abuse and Neglect, Washington, DC

Gladys Cairns, North Dakota Department of Human Services, Bismarck, ND

Marilyn Carey, Massachusetts Department of Social Services, Boston, MA

Sheryl Brissett-Chapman, Children's Hospital, National Medical Center, Washington, DC

Mary Jane Cotter, New York Department of Social Services, New York, NY

Christine A. Courtois, Private Practice, Washington, DC

Linda Darter, Georgia Department of Human Resources, Atlanta, GA

Howard Davidson, American Bar Association, Washington, DC

Vincent DeFrancis, American Association for Protecting Children, American Humane Association, Sun City, AZ

Martin A. Finkel, University of Medicine and Dentistry, School of Osteopathic Medicine, Stratford, NJ

Pat German, Harris County Child Protective Service, Houston, TX

William V. Griffin, National Child Protection Workers Association, Inc., Chapel Hill, NC

Judy A. Hall, Travelers Aid International, Washington, DC

Doris Harris, Queensboro Society for the Prevention of Cruelty to Children, Jamaica, NY

Norma Harris, American Public Welfare Association, Washington, DC

Sandra Hodge, Maine Department of Human Services, Augusta, ME

Loretta W. Kowal, Massachusetts Society for the Prevention of Cruelty to Children, Boston, MA

Dorothy F. Loftus, Delaware Department of Services for Children, Youth, and Their Families, Wilmington, DE

Elba Montalvo, Committee for Hispanic Children and Families, Inc., New York, NY

Betsy Rosenbaum, American Public Welfare Association, Washington, DC

Alvin Rosenfeld, Jewish Child Care Association of New York, New York, NY

Lynn Sanford, Forensic Interventions, Quincy, MA

Patricia Schene, American Association for Protecting Children, American Humane Association, Denver, CO

T. Jeanine Smith, Jewish Children's Bureau, Chicago, IL

Roland Snead, National Center for Child Abuse and Neglect, Washington, DC

Carol Springer, Montgomery County Department of Social Services, Rockville, MD

Robert Stein, Military Family Resource Center, Arlington, VA

Carla Strause, Florida Department of Health and Rehabilitative Services, Tallahassee, FL

Loren D. Suter, California State Department of Social Services, Sacramento, CA

Saul Wasserman, San Jose Hospital, San Jose, CA

Michael Weber, Hennepin County Department of Community Services, Minneapolis, MN

Major William E. York, Military Family Resource Center, Arlington, VA

Committee on Standards and Program Directions 1988, Board of Directors, Child Welfare League of America

Chair: Judith Sherman, Beachwood, OH
Vice Chair: Anne Duncan, Houston, TX
John C. Colman, Glencoe, IL
Marilyn Cox, Phoenix, AZ
Nan Dale, Dobbs Ferry, NY
Rick Fleming, Chicago, IL
Bennie Lewis, Kansas City, MO
Frank L. Oberly, Oklahoma City, OK
Norman W. Powell, Jr., Fort Lauderdale, FL
Lucy M. Sayre, Villanova, PA
Bruce W. Wert, Akron, OH
Regional Representatives, Committee on Standards: Jean Griesheimer, Worcester Children's Friend Society, Worcester, MA
Fr. William Irwin, Catholic Social Services, Edmonton, Alberta
Carmine J. Magazino, Graham-Windham, New York, NY
Jean Price, The Children's Home Society of Florida, Jacksonville, FL
Gene Svebakken, Lutheran Child and Family Services, River Forest, IL

Child Welfare League of America Staff

Robert R. Aptekar, Director of Standards Development, CWLA, Washington, DC
Beverly Jones, Senior Field Consultant, CWLA, Washington, DC
Emily A. Gardiner, Senior Consultant, CWLA, Washington, DC
Carl Schoenberg, Senior Editor, CWLA, Washington, DC
Carolyn Tucker, Senior Word Processor, CWLA, Washington, DC

HOW TO USE CWLA STANDARDS

CWLA standards are designed so that readers can quickly and easily obtain needed information.

A new, two-part format for the standards was approved by CWLA's Board of Directors in 1984. One volume, entitled *CWLA Standards for Organization and Administration for All Child Welfare Services*, presents the generic components of child welfare practice that apply across the field. All specific service components are presented in separate volumes and encompass only those service elements applicable to a particular area of child welfare practice. Each will be updated when appropriate.

The contents page provides a rapid review of the general areas covered.

For specific information on a particular practice, the index lists in alphabetical order each subject of interest and related categories in the text. Each standard is designated by a number. The digit before the decimal point indicates the chapter where the standard can be found; the digits after the decimal point designate its numerical order within the chapter. The introductory chapter, numbered "0," provides a historical background and philosophical overview and perspective for the remainder of the volume.

The first (nonindented) paragraph of each numbered section (excluding the introductory chapter) represents the standard. The rest of each section may be considered as elaboration, explanation, or illustration.

When various aspects of an issue are discussed in more than one standard, cross-references are noted in parentheses to other standards that are associated with or are part of the practice necessary for desirable service. Cross-references in service volumes referring the reader to standards in the generic volume are noted in parentheses by "O&A" followed by the digit (e.g., O&A:2.1). Cross-references in the generic volume referring the reader to standards in service volumes are noted in parentheses by the specific service standard followed by the digit (e.g., DC:3.1 or RCC:2.3).

Cross-references to the current eleven service volumes and the one generic volume are indicated by the following abbreviations:

A	=	Adoption Service
APS	=	Services for Pregnant Adolescents and Young Parents
DC	=	Day Care Service
FFC	=	Foster Family Service
GH	=	Group Home Service for Children
HC	=	Health Care Services for Children in Out-of-Home Care
IHA	=	In-Home Aide Services
ILS	=	Independent-Living Services
O&A	=	Organization and Administration for All Child Welfare Services
PS	=	Services for Abused or Neglected Children and Their Families
RCC	=	Residential Centers for Children
SSPF	=	Services to Strengthen and Preserve Families with Children

DIFFERENTIATION OF CWLA STANDARDS, COA PROVISIONS, AND LICENSING

CWLA Standards

The Child Welfare League of America standards are statements designed to be used as ideals or goals for practice in the field of child welfare services. They are intended to encourage the continual betterment of services to children and their families. CWLA standards carry no implication of control. Rather, they assist agencies in working more effectively, bringing collective experience to bear upon the work of each agency, both public and voluntary.

The standards present practices considered to be most desirable in providing the child welfare services that the community offers through various agencies, regardless of auspices or setting. CWLA's standards program illustrates one way in which a national organization influences practice throughout North America. CWLA standards make it possible to compare what is with what is considered desirable for children, and to judge the extent to which performance approximates or deviates from those goals. The standards are also intended to have an educational purpose in disseminating what is accepted to be the best current thinking and practice in each of the service areas.

Since CWLA initiated its standards-setting function, it has continued to revise established standards and develop new standards as new services emerge. Standards setting involves consultation with national experts and direct service practitioners, comprehensive literature reviews, and professional consensus based on knowledge and research.

The COA Provisions for Accreditation

Published by the Council on Accreditation of Services for Families and Children,

Inc. (COA), the Provisions for Accreditation are a set of requirements describing agency administration, management, and service delivery. The requirements are rigorous but realistic descriptions of practice that a competent provider agency should be able to meet. The provisions are based, in part, on existing CWLA standards. COA, as an independent accrediting body of social service agencies establishes a system based on measurable criteria. It represents a breakthrough in social service accountability.

State Licensing

Through licensing of child-placing agencies, residential group care facilities, foster family homes, and day care facilities, states and provinces exercise their police power to protect children from risks against which they would have little or no capacity for self-care and protection. Police power, as defined by Black's Law Dictionary §1401, is "the exercise of the sovereign right of the government to promote order, safety, health, morals, and the general welfare within constitutional limits and is an attribute of government using the power of the state to enforce laws for the well-being of its citizens." It is the basis of licensing laws. Licensing provides basic protections by the state or province for the well-being and protection of children.

INTRODUCTION

Belief in the need to protect children has developed in accordance with what society deems as the rights of its children. It is these rights that the community seeks to safeguard when it legally mandates intervention in situations involving child abuse and neglect.

0.1 Historical highlights

In 1875, the first Society for the Prevention of Cruelty to Children was established after the much publicized case of Mary Ellen Wilson. Mary Ellen was a young child who was treated brutally by her caretaker; she was frequently beaten with a leather thong and left without adequate clothing. A concerned citizen sought the assistance of Henry Bergh, founder of the American Society for the Prevention of Cruelty to Animals. As a result of the efforts of Bergh and other concerned citizens, Mary Ellen was protected and legislation was enacted to provide for the protection of not only this child but for all other children.

In 1909, evidence of society's concern for its children again emerged through the first White House Conference on Children. The focus of this conference was the family; subsequently, the United States Children's Bureau was created to "investigate and report on all matters relating to the welfare of children and child life among all classes of our people."

Concern for abused and neglected children was relatively quiescent until 1962 when the "battered child syndrome" was identified by Dr. Henry Kempe. With this stimulus came further recognition of the community's inherent responsibility for the protection of its children. This recognition led to such actions as the enactment of the Child Abuse Prevention and Treatment Act of 1974 (Public Law 93–247), the Indian Child Welfare Act of 1978 (Public Law 95–608), the Adoption Assistance and Child Welfare Act of 1980 (Public Law 96–272), and the Child Abuse Prevention, Adoption and Family Services Act of 1988 (Public

Law 100–294). These federal laws have provided us with a basis on which to builc a community program for child protection.

Over time, we have seen a growing public awareness of the problems of child abuse and child neglect. In 1972, it was estimated that there were 60,000 abused or neglected children in this country. In 1986, due to improved reporting standards, 2.2 million children were reported as abused or neglected. Between the years of 1976 and 1986, reporting of suspected child abuse or neglect has increased 223 percent. (American Humane Association, 1987).

Recent Developments in Child Protection

Society's commitment to and interest in the protection of its children continues to develop as our knowledge and understanding of child maltreatment grows. Recent evidence has led us to new concerns about sexual abuse, emotional abuse, and child maltreatment in settings outside the family.

0.2 Child sexual abuse

The reporting of child sexual abuse has significantly increased over the last several years. In the decade between 1975 and 1985, the official reporting of child sexual abuse increased by 1800 percent, resulting in an increased involvement of law enforcement officials. This has led to significant changes in the manner in which child protective service is delivered, including changes in some state and provincial laws and policies to mandate cooperative or joint investigations. (1.1)

Children, because of their emotional and physical dependency, are incapable of providing informed consent to sexual activities. Children are vulnerable due to the abuser's greater position, privilege or authority, age, physical strength, threat, use of deceptive or coercive techniques, or threat of abandonment. Child sexual abuse has a disruptive effect on children's physical and emotional well-being.

0.3 Emotional abuse

Canada and most states in the United States now provide a statutory basis for the emotional well-being and mental health of children. As our society has become increasingly knowledgeable about the effects of emotional abuse, evidence of injury to a child's development has become a cause for government intervention. Serious emotional abuse of young children can and often does lead to a failure to thrive. In older children, it can lead to a permanent residual impairment of physical, social, mental, and/or emotional capacities. Emotional abuse is a basis for seeking protection for a child. (1.1)

2

0.4   Child abuse and neglect in nonfamilial situations

Over the last several years, states and provinces have experienced an increase in the reporting of child abuse or neglect in settings other than the family (e.g., day care centers, schools, residential treatment centers). The community is increasingly concerned about violence against children regardless of the environment in which it occurs. Legislation similar to that governing emotional and sexual abuse has been enacted by most states or provinces, requiring community intervention in nonfamilial situations. (0.8, 5.3, 5.12)

Framework for the Standards

0.5   Basic principles

Children have a right to be free from abuse, neglect, and exploitation. Services in behalf of abused, neglected, or exploited children are based upon certain basic principles:

• the dignity of the child as an individual with a right to adequate care and supervision

• the right and responsibility of parents to protect children and to prevent their exposure to abuse, neglect, and exploitation (0.6)

• the responsibility of society to make available to parents the necessary services and resources that will support and strengthen their capacity to carry out their parental obligations to their children

• the desire of most parents to be adequate parents and the recognition that most parents are adequate parents

• the understanding that most parents who experience difficulty in parenting can be helped to be adequate parents

• the responsibility of child welfare agencies, as well as society as a whole, to dedicate resources to the prevention of child abuse and neglect and to educate the public about its effects

• the responsibility of society to provide adequate services and resources for basic needs (food, clothing, and shelter); the prevention of family breakdown; and the enhancement of the physical, social, and emotional development of children and their families

0.6   Rights and responsibilities within the family

In our society, both parents and children have legal rights that are accompanied

3

by corresponding responsibilities enforceable by law. Parents are responsible fo
providing their children with the love, care, and protection that they need; and fo
providing, within their ability and the resources available to them, all of the
following, until their children can care for themselves:

- necessary food, shelter, clothing
- adequate medical care
- protection and supervision
- moral and social guidance
- educational and vocational opportunities

Parents have the right to determine what happens to their children so long as they
carry out their obligations as parents. In making most decisions, parents are free
to follow their own best judgment. When a conflict between the rights of parents
and those of the child adversely affects the welfare of the child, however, the
rights of the child, as the more vulnerable figure, have precedence. When the
child's welfare requires it, the state, as the ultimate authority responsible for
protecting its children, assumes the right to intervene in regard to parental rights.

The rights of parents may be limited or abrogated by reason of parental failure,
harmfulness, or incapacity. The rights of parents, or those of the child, can be
limited, in their own or society's interest, only in accordance with due process of
law and only to the extent and for the period of time necessary to ensure the child's
protection. (3.9)

0.7   Response to intrafamilial cases of child abuse and neglect

The child protective service response to child abuse, neglect, and exploitation has
as its fundamental purpose the protection of children through enabling parents to
better fulfill their parenting role. The goal is to maintain and support the intactness
of the family, when appropriate, through the provision of services aimed at
stabilizing the family situation and strengthening the parents in fulfilling their
parenting responsibilities to their children. The guiding premise is recognizing
that most parents want to be successful, and through the provision of services can
be assisted in some of the following ways: (1) the development and application
of appropriate, nonpunitive methods of discipline; (2) learning conflict-resolu-
tion skills; (3) more effective interaction with their environment; (4) effective
negotiation with social support systems such as education and health care; and (5)
better understanding of children's developmental needs. Furthermore, as a result
of our increased understanding of the reasons for failure to carry out parental
responsibilities, support programs such as family life education, family support
centers, family preservation programs, in-home parent aides, respite care, or early
intervention by programs such as Head Start and parent-child centers, have been

4

developed to support families with child-rearing duties. Implicit in these approaches, and inherent in the approach of child protective service, is an understanding that most parents wish to nurture and care for their children, and that neglectful and abusive behavior is rarely due to deliberate cruelty. The proper intervention, therefore, is expected to be only as intrusive as necessary to assure the protection of the child, and should be ended when the child is no longer at risk of abuse or neglect.

This social service orientation to child protection is built into the laws of every state or province and establishes responsibilities for the reporting of suspected child abuse and neglect. Further, the state or provincial laws designate that there shall be within each state or province a public child protective service unit to serve as its legal vehicle for necessary intervention. When intervention is necessary, the legally designated public agency draws upon law enforcement, the medical community, the courts, voluntary child welfare agencies, mental health services, schools, parent aides, self-help groups, volunteers and other community supports. However, the primary responsibility for initiating the response to child abuse or neglect is legally vested with the designated public agency.

The role of the public agency is to (1) receive and screen reports of suspected child abuse and neglect; (2) conduct a comprehensive assessment; (3) determine if abuse or neglect has occurred and the level of intervention necessary to keep the child safe, and at the same time support the family; (4) develop and implement a treatment plan; and (5) evaluate the results and effectiveness of the treatment plan. In the United States, all of these efforts should be guided by Public Law 100–294 (The Child Abuse Prevention, Adoption and Family Services Act of 1988) and Public Law 96–272 (The Child Welfare and Adoption Assistance Act of 1980) which require reasonable efforts be made to help families reported for abuse or neglect before children can be removed from their homes and placed outside of their families, even if only temporarily. (4.2)

0.8   Response to nonfamilial cases of child abuse and neglect

Acts of abuse or neglect against children should not be tolerated by the community. Communities should work together to ensure that children are in environments that are free of abuse, neglect, and exploitation. These goals are inextricably associated with the broader aim of promoting quality programs in all child care environments. (0.4, 5.3, 5.12)

When abuse or neglect occurs outside the family setting, parents maintain primary responsibility to take such steps as are necessary to assure the protection and treatment of their children.

Parents may call upon law enforcement officials, licensing authorities, child welfare agencies, or other appropriate community resources in seeking the necessary protection and treatment for their children. The community, therefore, has an inherent obligation to make parents aware of, and to provide, a range of services to assist them in protecting and providing treatment for their children.

1

PROTECTIVE SERVICE FOR CHILDREN ABUSED OR NEGLECTED BY THEIR FAMILIES

A child protective service constitutes a specialized child welfare service for children who are neglected, abused, or exploited by family members.

1.1 Families for whom service is appropriate

A child protective service should be provided to those children whose parents, or other family members, are unwilling or unable to provide the protection children require, and whose condition or situation demonstrates observable evidence of the likelihood or actuality of injurious effects of this failure to meet at least the children's basic minimum needs. State or provincial laws provide legal definitions of the reportable forms of child maltreatment.

Children need protection from the following forms of maltreatment:

Physical Abuse. Physical acts by parents or caretakers that caused, or could have caused, physical injury to the child.

Neglect. Failure of parents or caretakers to provide needed, age-appropriate care including food, clothing, shelter, protection from harm, supervision appropriate to the child's development, hygiene, and medical care.

Sexual Abuse. Engagement by parents or caretakers of a child in any kind of sexual activity with a child. It includes, but is not limited to

forced or coerced sexual contact of any kind, exploitation through per
sistent sexual stimulation, child prostitution, sex rings, or pornography

Emotional Maltreatment. Parental behavior, such as rejecting, terror-
izing, berating, ignoring, or isolating a child, that causes, or is likely to
cause, serious impairment of the physical, social, mental, or emotional
capacities of the child.

1.2   Purpose of a child protective service

The purpose of the child protective service agency is to discharge society's
responsibility under state or provincial law for safeguarding the rights and
protecting the welfare of children whose parents are unable or unwilling to do so;
to assure that the neglected or abused child is protected against further harm; and
that the child receives the kind of parental care that will provide the essentials for
well-being and development.

A child protective service in behalf of a child is designed to assist parents in
recognizing and remedying the conditions harmful to the child, and to fulfill
their parental roles more adequately. If family conditions cannot be allevi-
ated, the agency must initiate action, either with parental cooperation and
consent, or through a petition to the court for a court order mandating
appropriate services for the child and family, or to obtain substitute care for
the child whose parents are unable, even with help, to meet their minimum
needs. (0.7, 2.5, 6.4)

Child protective service should also seek to identify and to advocate ways
to help overcome conditions in the community that contribute to or fail to
avert the neglect or abuse of children. (6.2, 6.3)

1.3   Distinctive characteristics of child protective service

The agency should recognize the characteristics of a child protective service that
differentiates it from other child welfare services. (2.1, 2.7, 2.8, 4.6)

In child protective service cases:

The request or referral for child protective service ordinarily comes
from someone other than the parents in the form of a report of suspected
neglect or abuse.

Many parents may be unaware of what is happening to their child, or
may be unable or unwilling to ask for or use help though they may
recognize that they need it.

In the majority of instances, services will need to be initiated by the agency in the interest of the reported child because the parents, or others responsible for the child, do not request the help they and the child may need.

Agency Responsibility in Child Protective Service

1.4 Responsibilities and duties

The agency designated to provide child protective service has certain defined responsibilities and duties mandated by state or provincial law. (1.15, 1.18, 2.2)

The agency is given the following responsibilities and duties:

- To receive, investigate within 24 hours of receipt of complaint, and assess allegations of child abuse or neglect
- To determine if abuse or neglect exists and if so, the level of harm to the child (1.8–1.13)
- To determine the capacity and ability of the family to accept and use help to remove the dangers to the child and to improve the present level of care
- To determine the level of intervention and types of service needed to protect the child and support the family's efforts to protect and care for the child
- To ensure that the needed services are provided
- To determine when and if court intervention is needed to protect the child and to file petitions as required

Reporting

The provision of a child protective service begins when an allegation of neglect or abuse is brought to the attention of the agency. (1.5-1.7)

It is inherent in the responsibility of the public agency to initiate prompt and effective action when children are known or thought to be neglected, abused, or exploited. A prompt evaluation of the circumstances should be made to determine whether a child is inadequately or improperly cared for, whether a child protective service is required, whether withdrawal or referral to another agency is indicated, or whether court action should be initiated.

In most states or provinces, reports of alleged child abuse or neglect emanate from two sources: certain professionals who are mandated by law to report;

and private citizens who may voluntarily report suspected abuse or neglec
(1.5, 1.6)

Mandated reporters generally include professional persons such as socia
workers, mental health professionals, nurses, physicians, teachers, chil
care personnel, clergy, law enforcement officers, and court personnel whc
in the course of their work, come into contact with children deemed to be a
risk or when abuse or neglect is disclosed to them. Nonmandated reporter:
may include the child, a spouse, sibling, relative, neighbor, or friend. In some
jurisdictions, all citizens are mandated to report incidents of suspected chilc
abuse or neglect.

1.5   Community reports

The agency should work closely with other community agencies and professional
groups that are in a position to identify children who are neglected, abused, or
exploited, and who can report such situations to the agency. The agency has a
responsibility to educate the community about abuse and neglect issues. (4.21)

The agency should develop agreements with schools, military bases, substance abuse treatment programs, American and native Alaskan Indian
tribes and nations, hospitals, hotlines, and other appropriate social service
agencies to foster preventive and outreach activities that encourage self-
identification by abused or neglected children and by abusive or neglectful
parents.

Where families are already known to others in the community, planning and
consultation with the organization that knows the child and family can result
in a careful determination of whether protective intervention or other
assistance would be helpful to the family.

1.6   Reports from private citizens

Citizens should be educated to make as factual and responsible a report as possible
and to expect the agency to respond appropriately. Anonymous reports should be
accepted by the agency. The agency should encourage reporters to disclose their
identity and inform those individuals who do identify themselves that their
identity will not be disclosed by the agency to anyone other than the necessary
agency and law enforcement personnel, unless otherwise ordered by a court.

The agency should accept the report if it indicates possible abuse or neglect
of a child, and should not ask the reporter to seek additional information
about the family to validate the report.

1.7   Inappropriate reports

Inappropriate referrals for a child protective service include, but are not limited
to, the following:

- Reports of child maltreatment of a person who is age 18 or older
- Requests for a voluntary service that have been incorrectly referred
  to a child protective service, including such services as day care, in-
  home parent aide, and family counseling
- Reports where information is insufficient to conduct an investigation
  (e.g., no information provided to locate the family)

If the decision is that the request, referral, or inquiry is inappropriate for a
child protective service, but some other service need is evident, the agency
should recommend to the reporter a plan of action that will meet the need
presented, and document that plan of action. If no other service need is
evident, the agency should explain this to the reporter.

Assessment

1.8   Receiving reports of abuse and neglect

In receiving a report of alleged abuse or neglect of a child, the agency should
assess the nature of the report, evaluate the source of the report, and explain the
agency's statutory responsibility, its services, and the available resources that
could be used in responding.

Staff members receiving reports should possess the highest possible professional skills by virtue of training, education, and experience. The agency's
professional response is critical to the child and the family, and to the
reporter's perception of the agency. At all times, respect for parents as
people, even if they have neglected or abused their child, should be conveyed
to those providing information. (2.5)

The agency should define, delineate, and interpret its services clearly in
order that the parents and the community understand the service, and why
and how it is provided. (6.4, 6.5)

Once a decision has been made, the reporter has the right to know and should
be routinely provided with the agency's decision, but confidentiality in
respect to the information received or given should be safeguarded.

Staff members receiving reports should have immediate access to any
information regarding the family's history of previous reports and other

services provided by the agency. Access to family history is a fundamenta
component of an accurate assessment of risk to the child. Confidentialit
should not be a barrier to gathering necessary information. (1.11, 1.12)

1.9 Response to report

The agency should develop standardized criteria for determining the most
appropriate response to the report. Because no child in danger should have to wait
for service, an immediate response is required and a child protective service must
be available on a 24-hour, seven-day-a-week basis.

If a report is particularly severe or complex, and/or it appears that the
involvement of the criminal justice system may be necessary, staff conferences or a multidisciplinary team to conduct the investigation should be
used. Formal interagency agreements should outline the roles and responsibilities of the various team members to minimize a duplication of effort and
demands made on the child and family.

1.10 Assessment of risk to the child

An initial assessment should determine whether the situation or condition of the
child requires a child protective service intervention, or whether some other child
welfare service may be better suited.

Throughout a child protective service process, including the initial phase of
evaluating a report and assessing the level of risk of harm to a child, the agency social worker should be guided by a standardized risk assessment
protocol.

The protocol should address risk factors and structure the decision-making
process to (1) assist the social worker in identifying those factors and persons
that influence a child's situation; (2) provide a structure for decision making
that offers continuity throughout the provision of services; and (3) provide
for increased agency accountability through documentation of decisions and
actions.

The following factors, at a minimum, should be included in the risk
assessment protocol:

- child factors
- parent/abuser factors
- family/environmental factors

Risk assessment considerations should:

- provide for the protection of the child as paramount
- assure that the most serious cases receive prompt and intensive

assistance

- support professional judgment, not serve as a substitute for it
- show sensitivity to racial, ethnic, and cultural differences (2.6)
- assist in developing the case plan, emphasizing permanency planning (2.4)
- include individual and sibling evaluations

Because of the nature of a child protective service and the potential of increased risk to the child during the assessment process, it may be necessary to provide additional monitoring, or immediate support to the family, to assure adequate protection of the child. Family supports such as in-home parent aides, respite care, or family preservation services should be thoroughly explored, with out-of-home placement of the child used only when necessary. (1.14)

1.11   Sources of information to assess risk

Parents should be a primary source of information, although other sources are necessary in the assessment of risk to the child. These sources should be sought out, with the parents' knowledge and consent, when possible and appropriate.

Other potential sources of information include, but are not limited to, professionals such as teachers, law enforcement officers, and physicians. Other community agencies, institutions, caretakers, or individuals known to the child and the family, such as relatives and neighbors, should also be consulted. (4.7)

1.12   Confidentiality

The agency should have a written policy on confidentiality to balance the privacy rights of the family with the need to obtain information to safeguard the rights of the child. (4.7, 4.11)

Confidentiality should not be a barrier to gathering necessary information. The agency's policy on confidentiality should be public information and formally shared with all participants in the process.

1.13   Results of assessment

Decisions based on the results of an assessment should be made in a timely manner. Time frames for making decisions should be set by written policy or regulation to assure uniform efforts.

A critical aspect of a child protective service is the decision, which may be vital to the child's life and well-being, whether to continue with a direct service, to withdraw, or to make a referral to another agency or service. The following procedures should be used in this critical process:

Disposition of the investigation of reports of suspected child abuse or neglect should fall into two categories: substantiated or unsubstantiated. While the term "substantiated" should clearly lead to some form of a child protective service intervention, the term "unsubstantiated" may be given for several reasons: (1) child abuse or neglect did not occur; (2) information was insufficient to determine whether child abuse or neglect had occurred; or (3) family could not be located. In some unsubstantiated cases where the child appears to be at risk of harm, services should be offered on a voluntary basis. The agency service information system should be able to differentiate among the various categories of unsubstantiated cases.

Insofar as possible, parents should be advised of the agency's decision.

The results of the assessment should form the basis for a case plan. It is best when parents participate in the case planning.

If the initial assessment confirms a risk of continuing or future harm to the child, the social worker, with the assistance of the supervisor, should develop a case plan to ameliorate the conditions that have created the risk of harm to the child. There are three ways to do so:

- Provide in-home support services to the family (0.7)
- Remove the alleged offender from the home either by consent or by court order (1.15, 2.7)
- Remove the child from the home with due process of law (1.18) 2.7, 3.3, 3.13)

1.14 In-home support services for family stabilization

The agency should have a continuum of in-home support services available, either within the agency or in the community, to ameliorate the risk of harm to the child. Appropriate support services should be available on an emergency 24-hour basis. (0.7)

The agency should identify service needs and advocate in the community for their development, adequacy, and availability. (1.17, 6.3) These services should include, but are not limited to:

- in-home aide services
- day care services
- respite care
- intensive crisis counseling (individual and group)

14

- medical services
- parent education
- mental health services
- substance abuse services
- family planning
- parent self-help groups
- legal services
- housing services
- educational services
- emergency financial services

1.15   Removal of the offender

If safety can be assured, it is preferable that children remain in their own home.

When the separation of the child and the alleged offender is necessary, an effort should be made to remove the offender from the child's environment.

The agency should have criteria and procedures for the immediate removal of any person and/or condition that constitutes a danger to the child.

Factors that should be considered in establishing such criteria should include, but are not limited to:

- the ability of a nonoffending parent/caretaker to protect and support the child
- potential risks to other children in the home
- the existence of substance abuse in the family
- the vulnerability of the child, such as age and level of fear
- the likelihood that the offending person will stay out of the child's environment
- the ability to alter conditions in the environment that endanger the child

If necessary, the child protective service social worker should cooperate with law enforcement personnel to see that the offender's absence is assured.

1.16   Factors to be considered with regard to short-term out-of-home services

When it is not feasible to maintain children with their families, the following should be considered: (3.13)

Siblings should remain together. (1.18, 2.6, 3.3)

Placement should be in close proximity to the family.

Suitable relatives should be given priority for the placement of the child.

The child's schooling should not be disrupted.

Sensitive attention should be given to cultural, ethnic, and religious characteristics of the child.

The child's placement preferences should be considered.

In all instances, placement decisions should assure an environment that will maintain the child's safety and be most able to meet the child's needs.

1.17   Emergency shelter services for children

An emergency shelter service is an important resource that offers both emergency protection for the child and an opportunity to provide stabilization. It is critical that the quality of care provided during this time be sensitive to the child's needs, and support the assessment and case planning process.

Emergency shelter placement services should:

- provide for admission on a 24-hour, seven-day-a-week basis, without regard to race, sex, ethnicity, or religion
- include trained, licensed, skilled caregivers who can attend to a range of children's developmental needs
- operate within licensing standards
- provide a caring, homelike environment reflecting adequate physical surroundings and privacy for the child during this period
- be time limited, not to exceed 14–21 days, allowing for the possibility of family reunification to be explored carefully
- provide medical screening for each child within 24 hours of admission
- offer specialized resources for the wide spectrum of admissions needing shelter, including older children and infants, sex offenders, substance abusers, and handicapped children
- maintain sibling groups where possible
- provide appropriate family contacts regularly, if possible
- recognize and respond to racial, ethnic, cultural, and language differences (1.10, 2.6)
- share vital information about the child with other professionals who may be working with the child during this time, such as psychologists, nurses, physicians, and educators

The child-placing agency should make available to the shelter any known

16

medical, social, and educational history on each child within 24 hours of placement and should maintain weekly contact with the child.

Child victims should not be placed in adult jails or detention facilities for juvenile offenders.

1.18   Removal of the child from the home

The provision of a child protective service represents government intervention in behalf of children to assure that their basic needs are properly met. The removal of a child from the home is a drastic act that should be considered only when there is imminent danger to the child's life and health, or when other measures to alleviate risk have failed or will not provide sufficient protection. The separation of children from their families has a profound effect on their lives; it therefore must always be a principal consideration in case planning. If removal is necessary, siblings should be kept together whenever possible.

The agency should carefully define the conditions that constitute imminent danger (1.16, 2.6, 3.3) to the child's life and health, which include but are not limited to the following situations:

The child has suffered serious physical or emotional injury, and the parent or caretaker refuses or is unable to protect the child.

The child is in a dangerous environment and there is a substantial likelihood that the child will be harmed, and the parent or caretaker refuses or is unable to protect the child.

The child does not have the minimum necessities of life, such as food, clothing, shelter, and medical care, and the parent or caretaker refuses or is unable to supply them, although financially able; or is offered financial or other reasonable means to do so and rejects them.

The child does not receive the age-appropriate minimum degree of supervision, and the parent refuses or is unable to supervise the child adequately, and providing services will not remedy the situation.

The parent or caretaker verbally threatens to harm or kill the child, or the child indicates he or she will harm himself or herself, and the parent does not take reasonable action to prevent it.

The determination of imminent danger must be made on a case-by-case basis, taking into consideration the child's age; the type of environment; the condition of the child; the behavior and condition of the parent or caretaker; the ability and willingness of the parent or caretaker to accept services; and the accessibility and availability of services and supports to alleviate the danger of harm.

17

1.19   Duration of child protective service

The length of child protective service in any situation should be determined [by] the nature of the problem, the parents' ability to use the service, and the progre[ss] that is made toward correcting the situation. (2.5)

An arbitrary time limit should not be set by the agency, but a period[ic] evaluation of the family situation should determine the proper focus an[d] direction of the social work plan and a prognosis on possible modification[.]

It is necessary to accept the parents' pace in using the social work servic[e] without losing sight of its main goal—adequate care and protection of th[e] child.

The intensity of the initial period of a child protective service interventio[n] is much greater than in other social services. This period must often b[e] prolonged so parents can begin to develop self-esteem and trust in their ow[n] ability to be more effective. As parents gain the ability to meet their child'[s] needs, the service can become less intensive.

1.20   Termination of child protective service

A child protective service should be ended when the child is receiving care that meets at least minimum needs, and the parents have demonstrated their ability to protect the child.

It is the agency's responsibility, not that of the parents or child, to determine when its purpose has been accomplished or is no longer needed, and at what point to terminate the service.

In a cooperative intervention, the other agencies and professional persons should be involved in planning the termination of service.

Service should be terminated if a report has been determined to be un-founded, even though no service other than the initial assessment and evaluation has been provided.

When parents have been motivated to improve their parenting and derive some satisfaction from their development, the social worker should clearly indicate to them that child protective service is no longer needed.

If the parents need and want help with other problems, the social worker should either refer them to an appropriate department within the agency or to another organization.

When parents have not been able to use child protective service effectively and the child's needs are not being met, or when abuse or exploitation of the child continues, the child protective service social worker has the responsi-bility to present the evidence and initiate court action (3.9), and service should not be terminated so long as the court expects the agency to monitor the child's in-home care. Service should continue if the child is returned home or if other children in the home require protection. If, however, the court fails to uphold the agency's assessment, child protective service should be terminated.

When a child is not receiving satisfactory care and the parents will not use the help, and there is either insufficient evidence or no possibility of obtaining evidence to refer these situations to court, the agency may decide to terminate its service for the present. It should notify persons who might subsequently obtain additional knowledge or evidence to report it at the time it is obtained.

2

SOCIAL WORK IN CHILD PROTECTIVE SERVICE

Social work with neglected or abused children and their families is the core of child protective service. Helping and supporting parents to provide the care that meets their child's needs is the most effective way to protect the child from further neglect or abuse and to promote the child's well-being. The purpose of social work is to help strengthen parents in their parental role, and to make use of the appropriate resources and services available in the agency and the community to assist them in doing so.

Social work provided in child protective service cases can range from brief service to long-term assistance involving the cooperation of other social service agencies, hospitals, and other community resources. It may require a complete range of support services. Social work services must be flexible, offering an immediate response to crises and a planned approach to chronic situations. (1.14, 5.1-5.14)

2.1   Child protective service as a specialized practice area

Social work in child protective service is a specialized practice area of child welfare, with many particularized features: (1.3, 2.7, 2.8, 4.6)

• A legal mandate requiring intervention, regardless of the parents' desire for help, that often causes fear and hostility

• An emergency-based service available on a 24-hour, seven-day-a-week basis

- The vulnerability of children and their inability to protect themselves
- The necessity to so integrate the helping and authority roles as to both intervene effectively and also strengthen families
- The necessity to collaborate with a variety of disciplines and community resources
- The coordination of actions in behalf of victimized children with law enforcement officials and the court system
- The directive nature of the service and its requirement that social worker make prompt and sound judgments and decisions
- The frequent needs of victims and their families for specialized treatment approaches

2.2 Authority of the social worker in child protective service

The social worker in child protective service should have a clear statutory responsibility derived from representing an agency with a defined legal responsibility for protecting children. The statutory authority should be complemented with the knowledge, skills, and experience of a professional social worker. (1.15, 1.18)

The social worker has the right and responsibility:

- To enter and remain in a family situation that warrants community concern
- To intervene in whatever way is appropriate to the requirements of protection
- To make clear that the community cannot allow a situation harmful to a child to persist
- To help carry out a plan with the child and family that leads to an adequate level of care and protection for the child
- To determine whether neglect or abuse has ceased and the service may be terminated
- To direct and coordinate all aspects of the intervention with the family
- To initiate action (even without the cooperation of the parents, when necessary) to legally remove children from parents and obtain adequate substitute care for them (3.9)

2.3 Social work methods

All social work methods may be used in providing protective service, including casework, family therapy, groupwork, and community organization.

22

In many situations, casework may be the appropriate and principal method used. This service is not exclusively clinically oriented, nor is it entirely dependent upon the professional techniques of interviewing or the use of the casework relationship. It is increasingly recognized that adaptations of traditional casework techniques are required in working with persons who do not express themselves easily in words, or who have not had the experience of having someone want to help them.

This service may require direct intervention with parents or children, individually or in groups, and the treatment of the family as a unit by social workers with specialized training, experience, and skills.

Since this service is intended to be supportive and remedial, methods may be used other than or in addition to those that are specific to clinical social work, such as teaching and guidance to help parents understand child development and behavior and to support them in anticipating and coping with the normal stresses and crises of family life and child rearing.

2.4   Case planning

The social worker should assume responsibility for planning the services to be provided, and for determining long- and short-range goals that must be achieved. (O&A:4.14–4.20)

Plans should be realistically related to the family situation; should safeguard the child and help the parents gain the confidence and capacity to care appropriately for their child; and should be flexible to allow for changes in the situation and the use of the services based on a continuing reevaluation of how the child is being affected.

The social worker should relate the plans to the community's expectations of the parental role and responsibility for children, and should work with or consult with other agencies, community services, and professions, as required.

The social worker should recognize that parents or caregivers who have mistreated their children, as well as the children, should receive treatment services.

2.5   Social work with parents

The social worker should maintain a constant focus on the goals of child protection in working with parents: that the child should receive adequate care and that the parents should be able to fulfill their parental roles adequately.

Social work goals will vary with different situations and at different times during the social work process. The social worker should aim to help th parents:

- Recognize and respect the child's need for and right to physical and emotional security; and at the same time, assist the parents to identif their own physical, sexual, and emotional needs, and how best to meet them in nonabusive and nonexploitative ways and in a manner that separates them from their child's needs
- Protect their legal and constitutional rights (0.6, 4.12)
- Mobilize their energies through the social work relationship and the use of other services, with the focus on improving their parenting skills
- Cope with environmental stresses and situational problems by locating and making use of resources and services available in the community
- Plan for the adoption of the child if this is appropriate (A:2.2, 2.3)

In a child protective service, the social worker should always be concerned with the needs and the protection of the child and with the effects of the family situation on the child. At the same time, the social worker should understand the stresses of parenthood and, in particular, the circumstances in each case that prevent parents from providing the minimum care necessary for their child.

The social worker should approach the parents in a manner that demonstrates a desire to help them provide adequate care for their child; a concern for them as persons, as well as for their children; and faith in their ability to change.

At the same time, it is necessary to make clear the protective function of the service and the legal responsibility delegated to the social worker to inquire into a report of neglect or abuse. (3.9)

The first opportunity to demonstrate that a helping service is being offered comes when the social worker tells the parents about the report and explains the agency's function. It should be made clear that if the report is substantiated, the social worker is prepared to work with them to correct the situation. The social worker should emphasize that the important thing is not who made the report, but whether it is true, and what may be needed to help the child.

The social worker should recognize and accept the parents' reaction to agency intervention, and help them express their feelings. Parents who are unable to acknowledge their expressions of hostility should be helped to do so nondestructively to avoid their taking out their unexpressed feelings on their children. Direct confrontation, with its implication of criticism, is not as helpful as giving positive support to the parents, who may more readily respond to the offer of a helping relationship.

The social worker must accept the challenge of being tested by the parents for trustworthiness, especially those parents whose experiences with other individuals and agencies have been hurtful and disappointing. As an authority figure, the social worker cannot expect to be trusted immediately. By focusing on the experiences and life circumstances that have meaning to the parent, the social worker can begin to build a supportive relationship.

Differences in ability to accept and use help must be recognized. Some families can accept help offered with sympathy and skill. Others may decide to use the service, although reluctantly or unwillingly, when they realize the social worker's concern for them, what the community expectations are, and further, that the agency is responsible for assuring that their child receive proper care. Some families can be best helped if the agency establishes an authoritative position and sets time limits that require the parents to work on those problems harmful to their child, unless they wish the child to be removed from their care.

2.6   Social work with the child

The extent and type of direct social work with the child should be determined by the age of the child, the nature of the child's problems, the child's capacity for understanding, the ability of the parents to help the child themselves, and the parents' willingness to permit direct help.

Social work with children is necessary to get to know them and to understand their experience, and to provide a continuing relationship through which they can receive help. This may require individual treatment by another professional within the agency, and continual monitoring of treatment progress and its implication for case planning and follow-up protective service.

Specifically, the purpose of social work with children is to:
- Determine if they are neglected, abused, or exploited
- Evaluate the effects of the mistreatment
- Ensure their safety
- Provide services to ameliorate the effects of the abuse or neglect
- Remove them from a hazardous situation when necessary

The social worker should see each child, as well as the other members of the household, in relation to the report and determine if problems are present for which help is needed.

If the child is hospitalized or identified in the hospital's outpatient program, the social worker should coordinate the investigation and follow-up with the hospital's attending medical and/or specialist professionals. The pace of the investigation should be based on the physical and emotional readiness of the child.

Whenever possible, arrangements should be made for the placement o children together when they cannot live with their parents. Children ma need support from the social worker to understand why they cannot be wit their parents at this time.

Social work with children who are alone, abandoned, orphaned, or removed from their parents and without receptive relatives, should access community resources and plan for placement in a temporary out-of-home care facility. For children who must be placed temporarily away from home, direct help can be provided in a relationship with a social worker who knows them and understands what separation means to children. The relationship may help sustain a small sense of security for the child, since the social worker is a liaison between the child and his or her parents and represents the known in a situation full of unknowns for them.

A full spectrum of evaluative and diagnostic services may be required to help abused and neglected children to understand the impact of the abuse or neglect and their subsequent treatment needs.

During the critical period of initial disclosure, services should be provided in a timely fashion by trained and experienced social workers. Each agency should maintain a screening mechanism for the identification of behavioral and psychiatric indicators that present a danger to the child or others, or subject the child to potential victimization.

The child should be the primary source of information. In collecting this information in an age-appropriate way, the child's right to privacy should be respected. (1.12)

Interviews with the child should always occur in child-centered environments and not in the presence of the alleged abuser.

To complete the assessment, the social worker should consult with other professionals such as physicians, educators, and mental health practitioners.

Every effort should be made to avoid direct multiple interviews with the child. The unique problems caused by multiple interviews should be dealt with through interagency agreements and protocols. Whenever possible, organized teams of extensively trained and supervised law enforcement officers, court personnel, and child protective service social workers, should work together to conduct joint interviews, or one interview viewed by others from behind a one-way mirror. The goal should be to decrease the number of excessive and redundant interviews. The child protective service social worker should remain a consistent and supportive figure as the child interacts with other interviewers.

All interviews should be conducted by skilled personnel who are sensitive to the child's racial, ethnic, cultural, and linguistic characteristics. (1.10, 1.17)

2.7   Law enforcement and child protective service

The agency should maintain a close working relationship with law enforcement officials. They should establish formal written interagency agreements that should include, but need not be limited to:

- cross reporting
- protocols for determining when joint investigations are appropriate
- roles and responsibilities of the respective agencies
- mutual training, with an emphasis on the dynamics of child abuse and neglect, services provided by the child protective service agency, and the legal procedures necessary to gain access to these services

In reports in which allegations of sexual abuse, serious physical injury, or death are made, the organization receiving the report (police or the child protective service agency) should immediately notify the other. The responsibility of law enforcement personnel should be in determining whether a crime has occurred and what action should be taken. As soon as possible, the child protective service social worker and the law enforcement officer should discuss their findings and jointly prepare further actions.

Any statutes, regulations, or policies that interfere with the freedom of the law enforcement agency and the child protective service agency to share information should be revised.

A law enforcement officer may be involved in protecting children in the following circumstances:

A court order has been obtained and the parents refuse to allow the child to be removed.

A child's life or safety is in immediate danger because of the parent's condition, and/or a family or household member presents a threat or danger to the safety of the social worker.

The child is behind closed doors and it is necessary to force entry pursuant to proper legal authority.

An act of abuse is being committed, or an act of abuse has been committed recently, and it appears appropriate that an arrest be made, or that the abuser be removed from the home.

When the agency needs the help of a law enforcement official, communication should preferably be with a specialized child protection unit of the police force, often identified by such terms as the Youth Division, Child Abuse Unit, or Sexual Assault Unit.

The social worker who is charged with the responsibility for planning for the child and the parents should accompany the law enforcement officer.

Law enforcement officials should be familiar with the social and emotional dynamics of intrafamilial child abuse and neglect.

2.8   Supportive personnel

Agencies should consider the use of volunteers and other personnel and define the tasks that they can competently perform as part of a child protection team.

Some methods of supporting parents in providing what their children need, or of helping families use community resources and support services, do not require professional social work knowledge and skills.

Under the guidance, direction, or supervision of a trained and experienced social worker, the following activities may be carried out by supportive personnel or volunteers:

- Assisting parents to acknowledge their need for help
- Serving as role models by modeling child care and home management skills
- Observing and monitoring a child or home situation
- Providing information about the community and its resources, and encouraging and helping parents to obtain a needed service or resource
- Maintaining regular contacts with schools or clinics
- Tutoring children
- Providing social and cultural experiences
- Providing accepting and supportive relationships
- Helping a child or parent to overcome social isolation

Use of Consultants

Services of medical, psychiatric, psychological, and legal consultants are essential in protecting children. Consultants should be selected on the basis of their specialized knowledge of child abuse and neglect, their experience, their ability to offer sensitive and timely services, and their willingness to collaborate with other professionals. (2.9, 2.10, 3.6)

Specialists and specialized resources should be available to the agency on a full-time, part-time, or contractual basis to meet the identified needs and problems of specific neglected and abused children and their families, as indicated in the case plan.

Consultants should provide information and professional support in their particular fields of competence to better enable social workers to use their knowledge and skills in serving children and parents. Consultation should not be confused with, or used as a substitute, however, for supervision that should be provided on a continual basis by agency social work staff members. Although consultation has an educational function, that should not be its sole purpose.

Consultation may be used to help define needed research, since over a period of time certain recurring problems may indicate a need for special study.

Consultation may be used in relation to diagnosis and treatment in particularly difficult cases.

The role of the consultant should exclude case management and decisions that are the responsibility of the agency staff.

Consultation should be integrated into the agency's activities and philosophy.

Consultation may be provided on an individual or group basis.

2.9   Medical consultant

The medical consultant should provide diagnoses of physical conditions, interpret medical findings, and provide advice concerning a program of medical care for the abused or neglected child.

The agency should select physicians who recognize their role in the overall therapeutic process and approach the child with the skill, sensitivity, and time necessary to:

- Develop a rapport with the child and parent
- Gain the child's cooperation and discuss willingly with the child the purpose and details of any examination before proceeding
- Allow the child to select an accompanying adult
- Allow the child to participate in the examination
- Conduct a comprehensive physical examination
- Formulate a comprehensive report with appropriate conclusions and recommendations required for medical treatment and follow-up
- Be available to testify in court as an expert witness

2.10   Mental health consultant

The mental health consultant should assist staff members to evaluate the child-parent relationship and the potential impact of the abuse or neglect on the family, and to give recommendations for the treatment of individuals and/or families.

Mental health consultants may include psychiatrists, clinical psychologists, social workers, or family therapists.

Consultants may also be used to assist staff members in managing job stress. It is essential that they be available in court.

3

ROLE OF THE COURT IN PROTECTING CHILDREN

Respective Roles of the Court and the Child Protective Service Agency

Child protective service agencies and juvenile or family courts share responsibility for the protection of children when their parents are unable or unwilling to provide for them. The ultimate goal of the juvenile or family courts and child protective service agencies is the same: to preserve the unity of the family wherever possible; and to provide for the care, protection, and wholesome development of children, separating children from their families only when necessary for the child's welfare. The security of the court and the agency that provides a child protective service should rest on the firm conviction that each has its own obligation to fulfill, and a fundamental responsibility to leave to the other its own functions as established by law.

The criminal justice system—law enforcement, prosecutors, and criminal courts—also has an active role in child protection. It is incumbent upon the child protective service agency to understand and work effectively with this system. Often, civil and criminal court systems will concurrently be involved with the same family. When this happens, the child protective service agency should help coordinate these systems so that the child and family are not unduly harmed by the competing purposes and values of these two systems.

3.1 Role of juvenile or family court

The child protective service agency should recognize that the juvenile or family court is responsible for adjudicating a case in which the legal rights of both children and parents are recognized and enforced. (3.9)

> Juvenile or family court is a special statutory court. An important function is the adjudication and disposition of cases in which the child's need for protection by the state is determined and due process rights for all parties are protected.

> These courts are protective in nature but judicial in function, bound by the rules of evidence, and inherently adversarial. They are required to assure that the legal and constitutional rights of both parents and children are duly considered and protected. (0.6, 1.12)

> The true potential of the court for the protection of children can best be realized when the court is presided over by a judge who has received specialized training and is specially assigned to hear such cases regularly.

> All judicial matters that relate to the same alleged abused or neglected child, including emergency placement, adjudication and disposition, foster care review, custody, termination of parental rights, and status offenses, should be heard in one court by the same judge.

3.2 Initiation of juvenile or family court action

Before the filing of a petition, the agency should have access to legal consultation. (3.6) Where the child protective service social worker and attorney disagree as to whether a petition should be filed, the decision of the agency should prevail, guided by the best interests of the child. Once a decision has been made to initiate court action, the petition should be drafted by an attorney, or by an individual under the direct supervision of an attorney.

> In filing a petition, the agency is requesting the protection of the state for a child. Specific and pertinent information supporting the allegations made in the petition is required in order that the court may determine its jurisdiction, the parents may adequately prepare their defense, and the facts alleged in the petition may be proven. In this adjudicatory hearing, rules of evidence are rigidly observed.

> In the dispositional hearing, all relevant material and information, as well as plans that the agency believes will ensure the best care of the child, should be offered as an aid to the court in making its decision. In the dispositional hearing, the rules of evidence are relaxed.

> Between the time of the dispositional hearing and the final resolution of the case, the agency may be called upon to provide periodic reports to the court

and to participate in periodic hearings. It should be prepared to do so in accordance with judicial requirements and sound practice.

The agency must be willing to work with the court for the benefit of the child before and after adjudication. Both the court and the agency should be clear about their respective responsibilities in each situation. The agency must follow any court order, or seek modification by review or appeal.

In seeking an out-of-home placement for a child, the agency must present to the court the clear and reasonable efforts made to avoid unnecessary placement, and the facts to justify a court order for such a placement.

3.3   Use of juvenile or family court in protecting children

When parents, despite the help that is offered, do not provide their children with the care and protection essential for their well-being, or when children are in immediate danger, action in the family or juvenile court should be initiated by the child protective service agency to protect the children. Parental rights may have to be limited, with the full benefit of due process of law, and to the extent and for the period of time necessary to make it possible to provide such protection.

The decision to petition the court initially, or otherwise seek a court hearing, should be made under the following circumstances:

The child is neglected, abused, or exploited and is in immediate risk of harm; that is, if a parent's action or failure to act is injurious or poses a severe threat to the child and warrants the protection of the court.

The child has to be removed from the home for emergency care, or for care away from the parents, because of conditions clearly dangerous to the child's physical or emotional well-being, and the parents are unable or unwilling to use the help offered to change the situation. (1.18, 2.7)

The child's parents, guardians, or other custodians are not able to discharge their responsibility to the child because of incarceration, hospitalization, or physical or mental incapacity.

The child has been abandoned or deserted and needs the protection of the court.

A judicial review of the legal status and/or placement of the child is necessary.

Some evidence suggests serious neglect or abuse, but the agency is denied access to the home, child, or other relevant sources of information.

After the court finds sufficient evidence to assume jurisdiction over the child, the court should consider the following:

- Whether the child may remain at home, with certain actions mandated to be taken by the agency and parents

- Whether the child may remain at home, and the alleged perpetrator ordered to vacate the home
- Whether the agency has made reasonable efforts to provide in-home services to the family (1.14)
- Whether placement, when necessary, is in the least restrictive manner consistent with the needs of the child and considers keeping siblings together, use of relatives, proximity to parents, practicality of visitation, and ethnic, racial, and religious issues (1.16, 1.18, 2.6)
- Whether the agency has made reasonable efforts to reunite the family after the child has been removed, or otherwise sought a permanent placement for the child pursuant to a written agency case plan

3.4   Use of the criminal court in protecting children

The philosophy of child protective service is to offer social services while protecting children. To effectively carry out this mandate, however, in instances where a child has been physically injured, sexually assaulted or exploited, or otherwise subject to risk of serious harm as a result of parental maltreatment, it may be appropriate to use the criminal justice system.

Child protective service social workers should have a clear understanding of the types of cases that should be referred to the district attorney for criminal action. These will most likely be cases serious in nature and committed with intent. Social workers should be aware of any statutes or policies that require referrals to law enforcement.

3.5   Use of the domestic relations court in protecting children

When there is an allegation of child abuse or neglect made in the context of a divorce-related custody or visitation dispute, the court has the responsibility to make an appropriate referral to the child protective service agency. When there is no reasonable suspicion of child abuse or neglect, a referral by the court is inappropriate. In no instance should the child protective service agency refuse to accept a referral for investigation because the abuse or neglect is being alleged in the context of a custody or visitation dispute.

3.6   Use of legal services

Child protective service agencies must have suitable access to legal counsel, and should use legal assistance routinely before initiating any court action or appearance in court. The counsel should be competent and experienced in child abuse and neglect litigation.

3.7 Use of expert testimony

A child protective service agency may suggest the use of a witness who is expert in court procedures to inform the court or to counter the use of expert witnesses by the other party.

A professional who is accepted by the court as an expert is allowed to draw conclusions from the facts presented within the court hearing and to testify to the general body of knowledge concerning child abuse or neglect or sexual victimization.

3.8 Testimony of children and parents

All children in court should be independently represented by both a court-appointed attorney and a court-appointed special advocate (lay guardian ad litem). Parents should be represented by an attorney. If they are financially unable to retain counsel, the court should appoint counsel to serve at public expense.

3.9 Helping parents understand court action

Parents should be made aware of each step of the judicial process through personal interviews or by letter in their own language or with the aid of an interpreter when necessary, whether or not they have been willing to work with the agency. The social worker has a responsibility to continue to work with parents even though an action in juvenile court has been initiated. Parents should be given written information that describes the judicial process in which they will be participating. The information should make parents aware of their rights in relation to the court, such as the right to be represented by legal counsel, to testify in behalf of themselves and their children, and to call witnesses. (2.5)

Parents should be made aware of the seriousness of the various factors that constitute abuse or neglect, as well as the responsibility of the community to protect its children from serious harm due to abuse or neglect.

When they have not been able to make the needed changes, parents should know that the matter may have to be referred to juvenile or family court, which is the legally constituted authority in the community for making decisions involving the welfare of children. Concurrently, parents should be helped to obtain counsel or to request that court assign counsel for them.

Parents' reactions and feelings should be recognized and supported. It is imperative that the social worker provide support to the family at this time. Failure to help the the family members deal with the reality of their feelings throughout the court process may result in additional difficulties for them as well as their inability to provide appropriate testimony essential to the protection of the victimized child. The decision to go to court may enable some parents to work on their problems more constructively. Many parents are afraid of appearing in court, fearful that they will be punished. Some may begin to accept the help they need as a result of the initiation of court proceedings, or they may begin to discuss what the court hearing means to them before, at the time of, and after the hearing, and this may facilitate their acceptance of services.

3.10   Working with the child

Any child who is old enough to understand the nature of the court proceedings should be told by the social worker what is being planned, and should be helped to discuss his or her reactions and feelings. (2.6)

The child protective service social worker should be aware of those aspects of any court case that may be emotionally difficult for the child and alert the child's guardian ad litem, counsel, and the judge to circumstances where the child should be excused from the court hearing.

In certain situations, the judge may decide to hold a private interview with the child to obtain information pertinent to the proceedings. The children should be told of this possibility, and their reactions and feelings should be discussed.

The agency should be aware of situations where it may be appropriate to have the child's testimony given through the use of closed-circuit television, videotape, and/or special hearsay exceptions. The social worker should discuss these options with the judge and attorneys.

3.11   Working with witnesses

In support of the petition, or any other matter under consideration by the court, the social worker should help legal counsel identify and prepare witnesses for court appearances. Together with legal counsel, the social worker should help witnesses organize their testimony concisely and accurately without biasing it. Since witnesses frequently wish to withdraw, special attention should be given to helping them understand the importance of their testimony in protecting the child. The social worker, together with legal counsel, should try to prevail upon the court to schedule the testimony of witnesses so as to minimize the disruption of their personal and professional obligations.

3.12   The social worker as a witness

Before testifying in court, the social worker should consult with legal counsel. (3.6) When social workers serve as witnesses, they should be familiar with the court procedure, the process of testifying, the responsibility that comes with qualifying as an expert, and the importance of responding to questions in cross-examination.

Social workers should have a clear understanding of Public Law 100–294 and Public Law 96–272, particularly the provision relating to reasonable efforts to prevent placement and to reunite families. The social worker should also be familiar with statutes and case law regarding confidentiality and the sharing of case record material. (4.7)

3.13   Participation of parents in placement

When out-of-home placement has been ordered by the court, parents should be encouraged to participate in the preparation of children for placement and in their adjustment to foster care. If the agency is aware of any special circumstances that require it, supervised visiting should be recommended to the court, otherwise, visiting should not be specially limited.

Parents should be advised in their own language of the terms of placement under the court order, and of their responsibilities and expected participation in the agency's case plan. (1.17, 2.6, 3.9)

The parents' participation can be important to the child in adjusting to the out-of-home placement experience. Although removal of custody from the parents temporarily limits their rights, they generally have the right to visit and continued responsibility to provide financial support. Visiting should be encouraged and facilitated unless clearly contrary to the best interests of the child. Service plans should be aimed at achieving permanency for the child as rapidly as appropriate. (1.18)

3.14   Victim compensation

Child protective service agencies should be knowledgeable of victim compensation policies and benefits within the state or province and assist the family to receive any appropriate financial support for crisis and treatment services.

Victim compensation laws should not contain language that in any way excludes child abuse victims and their families from eligibility for compensation, including compensation for the costs of mental health treatment services.

4

ORGANIZATION AND ADMINISTRATION OF THE CHILD PROTECTIVE SERVICE AGENCY

The goal of agency administration is to provide a framework for an effective service delivery system for children and their families based on the agency's legal mandate. Providing a child protective service is a difficult and challenging job with changing and often contradictory community expectations. It is therefore essential that the agency have a clear mission statement and a set of written policies and procedures. (O&A:2.1-2.3)

4.1   Authorization

It is essential that the child protective service function within the agency be provided through law or charter. (O&A:1.2)

Responsibility must be clearly delegated to the agency by law, or through charters granted to voluntary agencies by the state or provincial body authorized by law. It is advantageous for one agency to be responsible for providing child protective service to all who need it in the community so that there is no confusion as to where to refer cases, and the community can have a clear focus for its child protective service. The social service agency is usually the designated public agency for services to children abused or neglected in family settings.

Fundamentally, the public agency's responsibility stems from the will of the people to protect its children from neglect or abuse.

The publicly designated agency administering child protective service should have the duly constituted authority to receive and act on every report of familial neglect or abuse, and the right and responsibility to enter situations where its services may not have been requested.

4.2   Auspices

The state or provincial public social service agency, as the designated public agency responsible for child protective service, should assure that child protective service is provided to all children and their families who need it or for whom it is required. This may be done as part of its direct services or through purchase-of-service contracts with voluntary agencies properly authorized through charters, or a combination of both. (O&A:1.1, 1.10, 5.32, 5.38)

Advisory or Governing Board

The public agency designated to provide child protective service should have an advisory board of volunteer citizens representing the community it serves. Voluntary agencies should have a governing board representing the community they serve.

4.3   Responsibilities of the governing board

The board governing the voluntary agency shares responsibilities for developing policies, and for assuring the adequate financing and staffing of child protective service. (6.5) (O&A:1.24)

The board should:

- be convinced of the importance of a child protective service
- assure that the agency discharges its mission as authorized by law or charter
- assist in the development of policies necessary for the agency to discharge its functions
- provide a clear understanding of its role and the partnership the board shares with the staff
- be accountable to the community it represents, whether the responsibility stems from law or charter
- advocate for the needs of children and families that who require child protective services

- evaluate the programs of the agency in relation to changing community needs

4.4   Responsibilities of the advisory board

The advisory board of a public agency is responsible for being well-informed about the service; for making appropriate recommendations to the administrative authority when service changes or new policies are needed; for interpreting the service to the community; and for assuring good standards for the service through citizen action. (O&A:1.28)

Policies and Procedures

Policies and procedures governing the delivery of child protective service should be clearly written and grounded in the philosophy guiding the agency's intervention and treatment of families who abuse or neglect their children. They should be based on the legal mandate or charter of the agency and set forth consistent guidelines for case practice. They should include provision for staff participation in their development.

4.5   Agency manual

Policies and procedures should be written in a consistent format and organized in an agency manual available for use by the staff and by cooperating community agencies and other interested parties. Contents of the manual should provide staff members with a clear statement of their roles and responsibilities. (O&A:2.4)

A copy of the manual should be provided to each staff member for ready use as a resource document. The manual should emphasize the importance of consistent practice in child protective service. It should be incorporated as an integral part of the agency's preservice training program.

The manual should be organized according to the stages of the casework process and include a system for updating it and distributing new policies.

4.6   Specialized service

Because of the distinctive skills and responsibilities required in the provision of child protective service, it is imperative that it be located in a specialized unit when provided by a multiservice agency. (1,3, 2.1, 2.7, 2.8)

The need for specialization is related to the importance of urgent and constant concern for each child who needs protection. The responsible unit should be visible and accessible, and advocate in the community in behalf of abused and neglected children and their families.

Intake and emergency services should be available at all times, day and night.

4.7   Purchase of service

The public agency statutorily designated to provide child protective service should be able to purchase from voluntary agencies a wide array of services designed to protect children, improve family functioning, prevent the removal of children from their homes, and provide out-of-home care when required. Although services may be purchased from a voluntary agency, the publicly designated agency cannot delegate its legal responsibility for protecting children. (O&A:5.22, 5.41)

Services, or any combination thereof, that may be purchased include, but are not limited to:

- day care
- in-home aide services
- mental health services
- individual counseling
- marital counseling
- specialized sexual abuse treatment
- family counseling
- substance abuse services
- health services
- parent education
- self-help groups
- home-based services

4.8   Case records

Case records should provide a current and continuing account of the nature of the agency's involvement and social worker activity in providing service for each family. (O&A:2.22-2.33)

The case record should include identifying data, the source of the referral, the reasons for the referral, the outcome of the agency's investigation with clear documentation of the reasons for significant decisions, and the reasons for cases remaining open after the investigation.

The record should include a complete assessment of the family's functioning, a clear statement of the problems identified, and a service plan with goals and tasks to be accomplished within stated time frames by each person involved in the plan.

There should be a record of periodic reviews of the progress of the family in achieving the goals set forth in the plan. This should include documentation of the activities of the social worker, in particular, a record of information pertaining to the agency's and service providers' activities in behalf of the family and the family's interaction with the agency and service providers. This information should facilitate the review of previous case activity and provide information that may be necessary for court intervention.

Periodic review of each case, and summaries of progress, should be prepared for use in evaluation by supervisory and administrative staff. These summaries should be written within a consistent agency format developed in collaboration with the staff.

Because of the nature of child protective service, court action may be required. Therefore, accuracy and completeness must be maintained regarding dates, persons interviewed, content of interviews and descriptions of the home and the condition of the child. Documentation should clearly distinguish between facts and impressions.

Child protective service records should be separate and apart from other service records on the same family in a multiservice agency.

All records are confidential and should be kept in locked file cabinets or other secure settings. Access to written records should be subject to clear, written agency procedures.

Service Information System

4.9   Purposes

All states or provinces should maintain a centralized information system (known in some states as Central Registry). Preferably a computerized system, it should contain but not be limited to identifying data (date of birth, sex, ethnicity, name of parents, name of alleged perpetrator, address) for each child who is the subject of a report of child abuse or neglect; the type of maltreatment reported; the outcome of the investigation; the chronology and nature of services provided; and the outcome of the case.

The service information system should be used for the following management and administrative purposes. Identifying data should not be required to meet these responsibilities.

- To monitor compliance with legal mandates and agency policies and procedures
- To gather information in a uniform manner to facilitate management planning by providing statistical data on the characteristics of reported cases, the response of the agency to these reports, and the outcomes for children and families
- To obtain agency statistical information to ascertain the incidence of child abuse and neglect in order to influence public policy and legislation and obtain adequate resources for children and families (4.14)

The service information system should also be used for the purposes of case planning. It should include the capacity: (2.4)

- To determine if a reported child has previously been the subject of a child abuse or neglect report
- To assess the danger to a child by providing information on previous reports
- To maintain continuity of services when families move across jurisdictional boundaries
- To identify alleged perpetrators in order to assess the risk that they may present to children and prevent abuse or neglect of additional victims
- To accomplish these purposes, information from the service information system should be identifiable and retrievable by name of child, parents, and alleged perpetrator if other than a parent.

Identifying data on an alleged perpetrator in an unsubstantiated case should be kept on file with the information available solely for a subsequent child protective service investigations. If after five years there has not been another report of child abuse or neglect, this file should be destroyed.

4.10   Safeguards on use of the data

Service information system data should be considered confidential and protected by the state's or province's privacy statutes. Information on parents, other alleged abusers, and children should be safeguarded during and after any child protective service investigation. (1.12, 4.12)

Access to the service information system should be limited, with clear procedures for how, when, by whom, and for what purpose the information will be used.

The service information system should be used to screen applicants for employment in positions involving substantial contact with children, such as day care personnel, prospective adoptive and foster parents, and educators.

4.11   Expunging records

There should be clearly defined statutory criteria and time frames for expunging information when the report has been substantiated. State, provincial, and local agencies should assure timely compliance with their state, provincial, or local laws.

4.12   Confidentiality

State, provincial, and local laws should provide clear guidelines governing the practice of confidentiality and the permissible sharing of case information. It is important that the laws facilitate interagency cooperation, coordination, and communication to protect children and provide services to families. In cases where child protection concerns cross jurisdictional boundaries (e.g., the military, American and native Alaskan Indian tribes and nations, and interstate or international moves), written agreements and protocols should allow for the sharing of appropriate information falling within these confidentiality guidelines. Where state or provincial laws prohibit the sharing of information across jurisdictional boundaries, thus preventing the protection of children, child welfare agencies should advocate for statutory changes. (1.12 4.8, 4.10, 4.11)(O&A:2.28-2.33)

> At all times, the child protective service social worker has the obligation to maintain the client's right to privacy. During the course of an investigation, a social worker should use care and discretion in information gathering, while still carrying out a complete and thorough investigation. Violations of confidentiality statutes should be dealt with through appropriate civil and criminal penalties.

4.13   Right to appeal

The person whose name is entered into the service information system should be given the right to appeal the agency's process and findings. (O&A:2.11)

> Decisions or findings that are made by a court should be appealed through the judicial process.
> Child protective service agencies should inform families, in their own language, where abuse or neglect is alleged, of the agency's assessment process and of their rights and responsibilities during that process.

45

The interest of the child should be protected during the appeal process. Care should be taken to ensure that children are not further harmed or placed in jeopardy as a result of any appeal process.

Accountability

4.14   Use of statistics

The agency administering child protective service should use statistical accounting to maintain an accurate record of services rendered, and to identify recurring problems that have implications for community action. (O&A:2.19-2.21)

> The agency should know the sources, types, and classifications of complaints it receives, and the disposition of cases, including those not accepted for service. Statistics should provide unduplicated information on the problems and characteristics of the children and families served.
>
> Statistics should be maintained for specific purposes such as administration, community interpretation, and research. The staff should be able to see the results of the time spent in providing statistical data.
>
> Forms for monthly and annual reporting of required statistical data should present accurately the volume and types of services needed and the services provided by the agency. This information should be analyzed to determine staff and service needs, and to assess the individual performance of staff members and the effectiveness of agency services. Statistics should be available to substantiate the need for financial support for additional or new services, and to provide a basis for research into specific areas of practice.

4.15   Research

An agency administering a child protective service should either conduct its own research, or collaborate with other agencies to evaluate the efficiency and effectiveness of its methods and programs and to extend basic knowledge about neglected and abused children and their families. (O&A:2.34-2.39)

> Research concerning abused and neglected children and their families should use accepted research methodology and be directed by qualified research personnel.

4.16   Evaluation of agency program

An annual evaluation of the child protective service program should be conducted

46

either by qualified in-house agency staff members or by outside consultants. (O&A:2.5)

The evaluation should be used to assess program performance against established criteria and to modify or alter programs based on the results. A part of this evaluation should include an assessment of community service needs and the community's requirements for prevention and intervention. In addition, the efficiency and effectiveness of the agency's service to clients should be evaluated.

4.17 Evaluation of agency operations

Biennial evaluations of the agency's operations should be conducted either by qualified in-house staff members or by outside consultants. These evaluations should include an assessment of the adequacy of the agency's staffing, including number and qualifications of staff members relevant to the agency's mission, the adequacy of administrative procedures and systems, and the adequacy of supportive services such as staff training and the availability of consultants.

4.18 Review of child fatalities

Every child protective service agency should systematically review all deaths caused by abuse or neglect and all suspicious deaths in its service area.

Although the focus and protocol of the review process will vary depending on the number of cases involved, in all instances the review should be interdisciplinary and include representatives from the key groups involved in protecting children—social services, law enforcement, public health, the coroner or medical examiner, pediatrics, mental health, the prosecuting attorney, and child advocacy groups. By gathering epidemiological data and by carrying out intensive case studies, it is possible to identify ways in which the community can better protect its children and support its families.

4.19 Agency budget

The agency administering child protective service should develop a budget that represents at least the minimum funds required to render effective child protective service to the community. In the case of a multiservice agency, the budget for child protective service should be clearly delineated and distinguished. (O&A:2.12-2.15)

The community that holds the agency accountable for protecting its children should be responsible for providing the funds necessary to carry out this

mission and should require that the agency report on how these funds ar
expended.

4.20 Public accountability

Each state or province should have a mechanism for receiving and responding to
public inquiries and concerns about the capacity, responsiveness, and implementation of all services to abused or neglected children and their families. Large
municipalities may need to have a similar mechanism. This mechanism should be
sufficiently independent to enable an objective review of the inquiries and
concerns. It should encompass the roles of all parties who have the responsibility
for protecting children. (O&A:5.35)

4.21 Community relations

The agency administering a child protective service should interpret its function
and service to a broad range of community agencies and groups. (O&A:5.1-5.6)

> The community has a right to expect that the agency administering this
> service will make clear its function and the manner in which it is carried out.
> The agency should participate in defining procedures for referrals and
> cooperative services, including the development of written agreements.
>
> The agency should project a clear definition of its function to all persons with
> responsibilities for children who might have to make referrals to a child
> protective service.
>
> The agency has a special responsibility to make known its services to key
> groups in the community that are mandated to report suspicions of child
> abuse or neglect, to encourage the widest reporting of children who appear
> to be abused or neglected.

Social Work Personnel

> Child protective service staff members should possess those personal
> qualities, and the educational qualifications and competencies specific to
> their job, that enable them to work effectively with families who abuse or
> neglect their children.

4.22 Selection of personnel

Certain distinct personal qualities best enable child protective service staff mem-

...ers to work effectively with abused or neglected children and their families. The following qualities are most prominent:

- Recognition of and ability to set aside one's own values and prejudices in regard to special types of social problems and lifestyles encountered in situations of child abuse, neglect, and exploitation
- Receptiveness to the feelings and ideas of others
- Awareness and respect for cultural and ethnic differences
- Patience, good humor, and emotional stability in the face of crises and suffering

4.23 Professional qualifications and responsibilities of child protective service administrators

Administrators in child protective service agencies should have at least a master's degree in social work, and demonstrated competence, training, and experience in administration. They should have a strong conviction about the importance of the goals of child protective service and the ability to provide leadership to the staff, governing body, and community in accomplishing these goals. (O&A:3.4, 3.5)

Administrative responsibilities include, but are not limited to:

- Providing leadership in the planning, development, implementation, and evaluation of policies and programs, and assuring the quality provision of services
- Interpreting the service to the community in order to provide the necessary understanding of client families to other community services and resources, and to stimulate the required coordination and development of supportive services in the community

4.24 Professional qualifications and responsibilities of child protective service supervisors

Supervisors in child protective service should have a master's degree in social work, training in supervision, experience in child welfare and/or family services, administrative and teaching skills, and personal qualities that offer emotional support to staff members under stress and inspire the confidence of the staff and of the various community agencies with which the agency works. (O&A:3.7)

Supervisory responsibilities include, but are not limited to the following:

- Ability to assist social workers to assess cases objectively based upon the significant risk factors
- Ability to work with the community to identify families and children needing services and to coordinate these services

- Ability to teach new skills and clearly convey information to soci
  workers
- Ability to plan for and facilitate social workers' professional growt
  and development
- Competence in administration and personnel management
- Ability to communicate effectively with social workers and admin
  istrators regarding the respective needs and requirements of th
  agency, social workers, and clients

4.25   Professional qualifications and responsibilities of child protective service social workers

Child protective service social workers should have training in social work, and the personal qualities and capacities required in working with neglected or abused children and their parents.

It is important that the agency encourage social workers who do not have graduate training to acquire such training.

Social workers entering a child protective service should also possess the following:

- Conviction, interest, and confidence in relation to carrying out the responsibilities in child protective service
- Ability to assess cases objectively to enable decisions based on significant risk factors, using a basic knowledge of child development and family dynamics; and the possession of skills in interviewing, accessing community resources, and collaborating with other professionals
- Ability to organize, implement, and manage a case plan by providing, obtaining, and/or coordinating the required services
- Ability to use authority constructively to protect children and support families
- Commitment to continue the development of the special skills needed for providing child protective service
- Ability to work in a crisis service and to prioritize and manage multiple responsibilities

4.26   Professional growth and development

The child protective service agency should be responsible for ensuring that its staff members have the specialized skills and knowledge necessary to provide uality services. Staff training should be routinely available to newly hired ersonnel, as well as those currently employed by the agency. (O&A:3.19)

Training is effective only when it is provided on a continuing basis and designed to meet the identified training needs of staff members. Formal, organized training programs should be augmented by on-the-job supervision, job rotation, coaching, and self-directed training. The agency climate should be conducive to continual professional growth and development for all its staff members.

4.27   Career ladder work environment

The agency should develop a career ladder that provides compensation commensurate with social work responsibilities.

The retention of qualified and experienced staff members should be a goal of the child protective service agency. Toward this end, the agency should provide a work environment that is conducive to relieving stress and is supportive of its staff.

Emphasis should be placed on supporting staff through the availability of experts to consult on cases; through attendance at professional conferences and seminars; and through recognition of outstanding staff performance.

4.28   Workloads

Workload standards should be determined upon the basis of work units in child protective service, and should make it possible for staff members to carry out the intensive social work intervention required in situations of abuse and neglect. (O&A:3.2)

The following factors should be considered in the development of agency standards for workloads:

- The specific assigned functions and concomitant time requirement for each (e.g., intake investigation, court work, placements)
- The individual competencies of each social worker, including both skills and experience
- The extent of the geographic area served and the availability of transportation
- The availability of other services, especially foster homes, as well as in-home parent aides, and so forth
- The intensity of service an agency and community considers appropriate

- The number of other agencies or services involved in a famil·
  situation
- The amount of time a social worker is expected to spend on commu·
  nity activities
- The amount of time allocated to a social worker for agency activitie
  such as staff meetings, staff and professional development, and
  administrative functions

Every agency should conduct its own work analysis in order to determine its
appropriate workload standards for child protective service. In the interim
the following caseload sizes are recommended:

> *Investigation or Intake.* No more than 12 active cases per month. Each
> investigation should be completed within sixty (60 days)
>
> *Ongoing Cases.* No more than 17 active cases (families), assuming the
> rate of new cases assigned is no more than one for every six open cases
>
> *Combined Investigations and Ongoing Cases.* No more than ten active
> ongoing cases and no more than four active investigations per month

The ratio of social workers to supervisors should not exceed five to one.
Supervision in child protective service is critical to effective service delivery.

Caseloads should be maintained at reasonable levels. Any significant
increase in caseload size raises the risks to children, may result in poor social
work, and can lead to social worker burnout. Furthermore, the agency's
liability will be increased.

An agency may elect to create specialized units within its child protective
service. In deciding which approach to take, an agency administrator should
consider the benefits and disadvantages of specialization.
The benefits include:

- Greater efficiency and response to client's needs
- A more sophisticated level of skills and knowledge on the part of
  social work staff members
- Greater ability to respond to cultural and language differences

The disadvantage is a potential for social work staff members to lose
attentiveness to issues outside their specialized area.

5

PROTECTING CHILDREN OUTSIDE THE FAMILY

Child abuse and neglect does not always occur within the family or as a result of parental failure. Children are also neglected or abused by nonfamilial persons who are not necessarily within the home. When maltreatment occurs under these circumstances, parents have the primary responsibility to take such steps as may be necessary to assure the care and protection of their children. (0.8)

Children cared for in settings outside the home have the right to the full protection of the state or province. Incidents that do not involve the child's parent, guardian, or an individual who is continuously or regularly in the child's home should be considered as criminal issues and are the responsibility of law enforcement and the criminal justice systems.

Law enforcement and other criminal justice agencies should:

- Employ and support a skilled staff well-trained in the area of child abuse and neglect
- Receive, screen, and assess reports of suspected nonfamilial crimes against children and take prompt action to protect children
- Seek help from the child protective service agency and other service providers to minimize trauma to the child
- Assure that the protection of children is a top priority for not only the investigation and prosecution of child abuse and neglect cases, but also to assure that victims receive treatment

5.1   Corporal punishment

In all agencies providing care for children, including schools, corporal punishment should be prohibited by law and/or policy. (RCC:3.25-3.27)

> Corporal punishment is the infliction of physical pain for the purpose of discipline. There are many methods of discipline that are preferable, more effective, and safer than corporal punishment. All child-serving agencies should advocate for the prohibition of corporal punishment.

5.2   Compliance with state or provincial child abuse and neglect reporting laws

State or provincial child abuse and neglect laws should clearly mandate that all employees report alleged abuse or neglect in their programs to the appropriate law enforcement and licensing agencies.

5.3   Role of child protective service in protecting children outside the family

Where parents are unable to protect their children from nonfamilial sources of abuse or neglect, parental neglect may be present; therefore, the child protective service agency should intervene to provide the necessary services. (0.4, 0.8, 5.12)

5.4   Preventing child abuse and neglect outside the family

The best means of preventing child abuse and neglect in child care organizations is for programs to be well run and carefully staffed, accessible to public scrutiny, periodically evaluated internally and externally; and committed to parental involvement. Staff morale should be cultivated to ensure that there is an expressed commitment to quality care and treatment of children. The organizations should have adequate support and consultation, and serve a clientele for which they have appropriate resources and expertise.

5.5   Protecting children in public school facilities

Local school authorities should have written policies on nonabusive discipline of children, in view of a school's special position of authority and responsibility toward children. All staff members should be aware of this philosophy. (6.7)

54

When a child is abused or neglected in an educational setting, school personnel have the responsibility to protect the child by complying with the state or provincial reporting laws and by taking other necessary steps to support the abused or neglected child. Schools have a responsibility to cooperate with the appropriate investigating agency. Employment contracts should require staff members to comply with these policies.

Parents maintain the primary responsibility for the immediate protection and treatment of their children when and if they are abused or neglected in a school setting.

Law enforcement officials have the primary responsibility to investigate allegations of maltreatment in a public school setting.

5.6 Protecting children in governmental child care facilities

Governmental facilities should meet the same licensing and/or accreditation standards as voluntary agencies. Employees working in governmental facilities should be expected to comply with the child abuse and neglect reporting laws both when a child reveals previous maltreatment or in the event that a child is abused or neglected in the organization.

5.7 Protecting children in other licensed facilities

Where a child is alleged to be neglected or abused in a licensed child care facility, the public licensing authority has the primary responsibility for assuring the facility's conformity to licensing regulations that have been created to assure the care and protection of children. (O&A:1.5-1.9)

Parents and/or the child placement agency have the primary responsibility for the immediate protection and treatment of the child victim when the child has been abused or neglected in a licensed facility.

Law enforcement officials have the primary responsibility for enforcing the law to protect children when abuse or neglect occurs in a licensed facility.

5.8 State, provincial, and local licensing responsibilities

All licensing statutes should specifically refer to the requirement in the state's or province's laws that child abuse and neglect occurring in any licensed child caring facility or program should be reported to local law enforcement officials, and the agency licensing that facility or program.

Licensing presents a major opportunity to prevent the maltreatment of children in out-of-home care or placement settings. Through licensing, standards can be set and enforced relative to those who provide care, as well as to the environment in which care is given. For this reason, concern about programs that are not licensed or are not currently required to be licensed is justified. Legislation should be enacted to remedy these omissions.

Following the completion of an investigation into allegations of child abuse or neglect, the licensing agency should establish a definitive plan with the licensee to correct any deficiencies in the setting that were identified in the investigation as contributing to an unsatisfactory environment for children. The licensing agency should monitor the implementation of this plan and notify the licensee when it has been successfully completed.

Not all allegations of child abuse or neglect are, in and of themselves, of such a serious nature as to require immediate action, but the licensing agency should be able to take whatever action is necessary to protect the health, safety, and welfare of children. All licensing agencies should have the authority to suspend or revoke a license immediately upon an initial finding that children are in danger.

5.9 Prelicensure and preemployment checks

The screening of potential licensees and employees is an important step in ensuring the safety of children. An array of preemployment and prelicensure checks should be used, and should include criminal background checks obtained through state or provincial or federal law enforcement agencies. Criminal background checks should be carried out with adequate protections for confidentiality and an individual's civil rights.

Preemployment and prelicensure checks should not be viewed as a guarantee of the safety of children. Systematic and continued attention should be given to the quality of the staff in child-serving settings, not only in the hiring process, but also by providing continuing supervision, as well as mandatory training.

5.10 Past criminal or child protective service records

It is essential to screen from licensure or employment those individuals with criminal records that include substantiated child abuse or neglect.

This should be accomplished through employment application procedures that directly seek information regarding past records and through police criminal record checks.

The following questions should be asked:

Has the applicant ever been convicted of any crime of violence against a person, crime against children, or a sexual offense against children, or is the applicant currently charged with any such crime?

Is the applicant currently under investigation by a law enforcement or child protective service agency for child abuse or neglect, or assault on a child?

Has the applicant been the recipient of a dispositional finding of substantiated child abuse or neglect as a result of an investigation into one of these alleged acts?

These questions should be included by the licensing agency in its application for licensure. In addition, the questions should be used by licensees (e.g., day care centers, residential facilities) in their hiring of staff members and in their screening of volunteers. The questions are intended to be asked of all individuals who provide care to children.

The questions seek information about pending criminal charges as well as actual convictions. This is important because criminal background checks will disclose only convictions. It is important for an individual seeking licensure to disclose pending charges as well, so that a licensor or employer may evaluate whether the information could affect the applicant's ability to care for children.

The types of offense referred to in these questions are those that may indicate potential problems in someone caring for children. An affirmative answer to these questions should not be an automatic bar to licensure or employment. For example, there could be instances of previous criminal behavior (e.g., drunken driving where an individual has been sober for many years) that may not affect an individual's current ability to care for children. This information should be part of the evaluation of an applicant's suitability for employment. Decision making should reflect a balance between the legitimate need to protect children and the desire to avoid unnecessary denial of employment to an individual. The rationale for employment decisions should be documented.

5.11 Previous employers and other references

All licensor and employers should require applicants to submit the names and addresses of previous employers, as well as other references. Checks of reference should inquire if they know of any reason why the applicant should not work in a setting in which children are receiving care. (5.9)

All actions made in checking references should be documented in the licensure or employment records.

5.12 Nonemployed adults present in the child care setting

Licensing agencies should be concerned about all individuals, besides the licensee and employees, who are present in the child care setting at the time the service is provided.

Often incidents of child abuse or neglect in settings outside the family are committed by others present in the child care setting. Of particular concern are minors who have a history of physical or sexual aggression.

Any nonemployed adult who will be present regularly in a child care setting during the time children are present should be asked prior to licensure, or as a condition of continued licensure, whether he or she:

- Has ever been convicted of any crime of violence, crime against children, or sexual offense of any type
- Has ever been charged with any crime of violence, crime against children, or sexual offense of any type
- Is currently the subject of a child abuse or neglect investigation
- Has ever been the recipient of a finding of substantiated child abuse or neglect by a child protective service agency as a result of an investigation into one of these alleged acts

5.13 Staff training

Training should be used as an essential element in the prevention of child abuse and neglect in child-serving agencies. Assistance from staff members of the child protective service agency should be solicited for the development and presentation of the child abuse and neglect components of this training. To be effective, training should not be a one-time program; rather, it should be a part of an ongoing staff development process. (4.26)(O&A:3.19)

Agencies that license child care settings should mandate that licensees and employees be trained in:

- The statutes and regulations pertinent to the setting's licensing and employment requirements regarding child abuse and neglect reporting
- Childhood development
- Practices for assuring quality care in the particular child care setting

5.14 Program monitoring

All agencies that administer, license, and/or regulate programs that care for children outside of their own homes should provide for the timely and consistent

58

monitoring of the settings they are concerned with, and, in particular, should provide for such monitoring on-site, at least annually, and unannounced when warranted.

Monitoring, the periodic and regular review of a program, is necessary to ensure quality care of children. It is the means by which programs are held accountable for providing the service they purport to offer.

Although unannounced visits may cause concern for operating agencies, the capacity and opportunity to conduct such visits must exist. This is particularly important when there is an indication that a problem exists.

6

PROTECTING CHILDREN: AN INHERENT COMMUNITY RESPONSIBILITY

Protecting children is a community responsibility. All segments of the community should be made aware of their appropriate responsibilities. Although parents have the primary responsibility to protect their children, child welfare agencies, both public and voluntary, share a responsibility to support parents by providing assertive and continual leadership within their communities to mobilize the community's resources, not only to meet the needs of their own clients, but also those of all children. Collectively, each community has an obligation to ensure that the required services and resources are available for the prevention, intervention, and treatment of child abuse and neglect.

6.1   Role of parents

Parents have the primary responsibility to ensure that their children are protected from abuse, neglect, and exploitation both within the family and within organizations that care for their children.

To meet this obligation, parents should:
- Provide adequate care and supervision of their children
- Learn and apply appropriate, nonpunitive disciplinary techniques
- Involve themselves in the activities of agencies serving their child
- Seek help whenever it is appropriate

Parents often are in the best position to recognize and identify possible signs of child abuse and neglect. Whether intervention and treatment occur, depends upon the parents' willingness and ability to report their observations to the appropriate agency.

To fulfill this responsibility, parents should:

- Be aware of and sensitive to the signs of possible child abuse and neglect
- Initiate action to protect their child by filing a report of suspected child abuse or neglect with the appropriate agency
- Take the steps necessary to mitigate any damage that the child may have suffered
- Support the child during the process of evaluating the allegations, including cooperation with the appropriate authorities during the investigative process
- Participate in the development and implementation of a treatment plan for the child and family

6.2   Role of community networks

Networks, composed of parents and those agencies and individuals working with children and their families, should be developed in every community to improve services and resources for victimized children and their families. (1.12, 6.3)

The community network should include, but not be limited to, parents, the designated child protective service agency, representatives of public and voluntary child welfare and other social agencies, health and mental health agencies, the courts, law enforcement groups, the schools, substance abuse treatment programs, American Indian and Alaskan native tribes and nations, and the military.

The network's responsibilities should include prevention, case identification, reporting, assessment, treatment, and advocacy. All agencies concerned about children and families should be encouraged to participate in this communitywide effort to advocate for and address conditions that may cause or increase child abuse and neglect. This means the inclusion of all institutions within the community, including the schools, churches, civic groups, health agencies, businesses, and private citizens.

Specifically, community networks should:

- Assist in developing working agreements among the various agencies involved in providing services to children who are neglected, abused, or exploited

- Interpret to the community the function and tasks necessary to protect children
- Stimulate public interest in the conditions whose inadequacy is associated with child abuse and neglect, such as housing, education, public assistance, child labor laws, social and health services
  - Advocate for the development of new community services and approaches that will be effective in preventing families from neglecting or abusing their children
  - Organize a communitywide effort for case identification and reporting
  - Develop a coordinated effort for the intervention and treatment of victimized children and their families

6.3 Advocacy in behalf of vulnerable children and families

Child welfare agencies should advocate to protect the community's vulnerable children by providing the leadership necessary to create and/or participate in a community network of concerned agencies and individuals. (1.2, 6.2)

Communitywide advocacy activities of child welfare agencies should include:

- Conducting public awareness campaigns to inform all segments of the community of the extent and nature of child abuse and neglect and the resources necessary to prevent it, as well as those required to protect children and strengthen families
- Cooperating with all community child-serving agencies and individuals able and willing to work on preventing child abuse and neglect, and assisting victimized children and their families
- Developing needed new resources and services to meet the protection needs of all children and their families, using federal, provincial or state, local, and private sources of funding

Role of Agencies Serving Children and Their Families

Agencies serving children and their families should participate in the community network by galvanizing the support of parents, professionals, and other child-serving agencies within their community to pursue a comprehensive agenda for preventing child abuse and neglect. Roles for the various segments of the community are described below.

6.4   Role of the child protective service agency

The state or provincial agency designated to provide child protective service has the public responsibility to act for the community in ensuring that children are protected from harm by their parents or guardians. The agency's intervention should be delivered in a manner that not only provides safety for the children, but also seeks to ameliorate those conditions that led to the abuse or neglect. (1.4, 6.11)

To achieve these goals, the agency should engage in the following activities:

- Receiving, screening, and assessing reports of suspected child abuse and neglect and taking prompt action to protect children
- Providing for a 24-hour, seven-day-a-week response capability using a multidisciplinary approach
- Employing and supporting a skilled and well-trained staff
- Assuring protection of children and their siblings by either providing in-home services to families, or seeking removal of the victimized child or abuser with court approval
- Maintaining a child-centered, family-focused approach during all phases of the treatment services
- Involving relevant community resources in the development, implementation, and monitoring of case plans
- Developing written interagency agreements with the criminal justice system delineating the roles and responsibilities of each agency in criminal matters
- Involving children and their families in the development and implementation of the case plan, including transfers or discharge of cases
- Developing memoranda of understanding or contracts with out-of-home care providers to ensure a smooth transition for children and families where necessary, and working toward the reunification of families wherever possible
- Advocating for appropriate and sufficient services for abused and neglected children, their siblings, and parents

6.5   Role of the voluntary child-serving agency governing board

The governing board of a voluntary child welfare or other voluntary child-serving agency should be responsible for assuring that its programs operate in a violence-free environment. (4.3)

Toward this end, the board should:

- Assure that its service programs promote healthy child development and respond to the needs of individual children
- Assure that staff members who work with children are properly screened and trained in the problems of child abuse and neglect
- Assure that the agency has a written protocol for the reporting of child abuse and neglect to the appropriate authorities (5.2)
- Assure that there are written agreements with the designated public child protective service agency, law enforcement agency, and other appropriate agencies regarding the identification, reporting, and treatment of child abuse and neglect
- Assure that there are policies and practices for identifying and responding to high-risk situations
- Assure that children in their programs are treated humanely and with respect
- Advocate for children and their basic needs
- Collect and disseminate information about the types and incidence of child abuse and neglect
- Develop discipline policies that prohibit corporal, humiliating, or degrading punishment. (RCC:3.25-3.27)

6.6   Role of mental health and medical care practitioners

Mental health and medical care practitioners should work with individual families and cooperatively with other community agencies to provide appropriate care and support and to prevent and/or to treat child abuse and neglect. (1.14, 2.9, 2.10)

These professionals should participate in:
- Conducting aggressive outreach efforts to high-risk children and their families
- Providing parenting education and support in stress reduction and the promotion of positive physical and mental health
- Multidisciplinary teams
- Assisting victimized children and their families by providing treatment services and follow-up care
- Training staff members in the identification of high-risk factors for child abuse and neglect, and in effective, appropriate professional responses
- Facilitating collaboration among all child-serving agencies and individuals

6.7   Role of schools

All school districts, in recognition of their special position of authority and responsibility in relation to children, should have written policies related to the respectful treatment of children. Every local board of education should accept responsibility for assuring that the schools within their jurisdiction conform to those policies and for providing an environment that assures the care and protection of children. (5.5)

Elementary and secondary schools, as part of their educational program, should:

- Support parenting education classes
- Offer child safety courses
- Provide before and after school child day care
- Train staff members in the identification of both the high-risk factors and indicators of child abuse and neglect
- Train staff members in effective and appropriate methods of managing students in the classroom
- Advocate for policies prohibiting corporal punishment

Institutions of higher education should play a significant role in the prevention and treatment of child abuse or neglect.

The following are activities in which colleges or universities should participate:

- Provision of such volunteer services as research, clinical social work, and consultation
- Advocacy for quality services to children in the community in which they are located
- Education of students and practitioners in all related fields (such as social work, medicine, and law) in the state-of-the-art issues regarding child abuse and neglect

6.8   Role of social and religious organizations

Associations, churches, synagogues, and other voluntary social and religious child-serving organizations should be actively involved in the prevention of child abuse or neglect.

These organizations should participate in such activities as:

- Supporting self-help groups
- Participating in advocacy efforts to support adequate family assistance programs, such as employment services, housing, day care, and income maintenance

- Sponsoring programs that promote the healthy development of children, such as recreational activities, camps, and healthy family life education
- Training staff members in the identification of both high-risk factors and the indicators of child abuse and neglect
- Increasing the awareness and understanding of child abuse and neglect, and the issues that stress family needs in the local community

6.9   Role of business

Business should play a significant role in supporting parents employed by them, and thereby contribute to the prevention of child abuse or neglect. (DC:1.7) (O&A:5.29)

Activities to promote this effort should include:

- Providing corporate-sponsored day care programs, including after-school programs, flextime for employees who require it, and parental leave
- Advocating for programs within the corporate structure that enhance family life
- Developing employee assistance programs

6.10   Role of the media

The media should assist the community in its efforts to prevent and treat child abuse or neglect through such activities as:

- Developing an understanding of the dynamics of child abuse and neglect
- Seeking a balanced perspective whenever reporting on this topic
- Assuring that media presentations do not exploit children
- Developing community standards and ethics in conjunction with professional agencies regarding the presentation of child abuse and neglect issues

6.11   Role of licensing agency

Licensing agencies have a major responsibility to prevent the abuse and neglect of children in out-of-home care or placement settings and should possess the authority to take prompt and decisive action to protect children.

To this end, licensing agencies should provide activities such as:

- Training licensing staff members in the area of child abuse and neglect
- Assuring that licensing standards are adequate for the safety and well-being of children
- Collecting and disseminating information about the safety and the well-being of children, as well as the epidemiological trends on which future licensing planning and directions can be based
- Assuring that licensed facilities have written policies on the reporting of child abuse and neglect
- Responding to all reports of child abuse and neglect in any licensed facility
- Seeing that deficiencies noted in the course of an investigation of a licensed agency are corrected in a timely manner
- Consulting with the designated public child protective service agency and law enforcement agency during an investigation of suspected child abuse and neglect
- Taking prompt action to assure the safety of children

6.12 Role of credentialing authorities

Groups that credential practitioners should have the responsibility of informing and educating their professionals about the complex issues and professional responsibilities related to child abuse and neglect.

Credentialing authorities can engender increased support for needed services to children and their families by:

- Assuring that their professionals comply with the mandatory reporting law in their states or provinces
- Taking prompt action against those professionals who failed to report suspected child abuse and neglect
- Supporting the principle that the reporting of abuse or neglect is an inherent part of the process of helping children and their families.

SELECTED REFERENCES

Alter, Catherine Foster. "Decision-Making Factors in Cases of Child Neglect." *Child Welfare* LXIV, 2 (March–April 1985): 99–111.

American Humane Association. *Highlights of Official Child Neglect and Abuse Reporting 1986.* Denver, CO: American Humane Association, 1988.

Antler, Stephen, ed. *Child Abuse and Child Protection: Policy and Practice.* Silver Spring, MD: National Association of Social Workers, 1982.

Bell, Cynthia J. "Working with Child Witnesses." *Public Welfare* 46, 1 (Winter 1988): 5–13.

Besharov, Douglas J., ed. *Child Abuse and the Law: A Canadian Perspective.* Washington, DC: Child Welfare League of America, 1985.

———. "Policy Guidelines for Decision Making in Child Abuse and Neglect." *Children Today* 16, 6 (November–December 1987): 7–10, 33.

———. "Putting Central Registers to Work." *Children Today* 6, 5 (September–October 1977): 9–13.

———. *The Vulnerable Social Worker: Liability for Serving Children and Families.* Silver Spring, MD: National Association of Social Workers, 1985.

Borgman, Robert. "Antecedents and Consequences of Parental Rights Termination for Abused and Neglected Children." *Child Welfare* LX, 6 (June 1981): 391–404.

Bourne, Richard, and Newberger, Eli H., eds. *Critical Perspectives on Child Abuse.* Lexington, MA: D.C. Heath and Company, 1979.

Caulfield, Barbara A. *Child Abuse and the Law: A Legal Primer for Social Workers.* Chicago: National Committee for Prevention of Child Abuse, 1979.

Caulfield, Barbara A. *Legal Aspects of Protective Services for Abused and Neglected Children: A Manual.* Washington, DC: U.S. Department of Health, Education, and Welfare, (OHDS), Administration for Public Services, 1978.

Conte, Jon R. "The Justice System and Sexual Abuse of Children." *Social Service Review* 58, 4 (December 1984): 556–568.

Copans, Stuart; Krell, Helen; Gundy, John H.; Rogan, Janet; and Field, Frances. "The Stresses of Treating Child Abuse." *Children Today* 8, 1 (January–February 1978): 22–27, 35.

Dale, Peter, with Davies, Murray, Morrison, Tony, and Waters, Jim. *Dangerous Families: Assessment and Treatment of Child Abuse.* New York: Tavistock Publications, 1986.

DiLeonardi, Joan W. "Decision Making in Protective Services." *Child Welfare* LIX, 6 (June 1980): 356–364.

Ebeling, Nancy B., and Hill, Deborah A. *Child Abuse and Neglect: A Guide with Case Studies for Treating the*

Child and Family. Littleton, MA: Wright-PSG Inc., 1983.

Ellenson, Gerald S. "Detecting a History of Incest: A Predictive Syndrome." *Social Casework* 66, 9 (November 1985): 525–532.

Elmer, Elizabeth. *Fragile Families, Troubled Children: The Aftermath of Infant Trauma.* Pittsburgh, PA: University of Pittsburgh Press, 1978.

Falconer, Nancy E., with Swift, Karen. *Preparing for Practice: The Fundamentals of Child Protection.* Toronto, Ontario, Canada: Children's Aid Society of Metropolitan Toronto, 1980.

Faller, Kathleen Coulborn, ed. *Social Work with Abused and Neglected Children: A Manual of Interdisciplinary Practice.* New York: The Free Press, 1981.

Finkelhor, David. *Child Sexual Abuse: New Theory and Research.* New York, NY: The Free Press, 1984.

Fontana, Vincent J., and Besharov, Douglas J. *The Maltreated Child: The Maltreatment Syndrome in Children—A Medical, Legal, and Social Guide.* 4th ed. Springfield, IL: Charles C. Thomas, 1979.

Garbarino, James; Guttmann, Edna; and Wilson Seeley, Janis. *The Psychologically Battered Child: Strategies for Identification, Assessment, and Intervention.* San Francisco, CA: Jossey-Bass Inc., 1986.

———, and Stocking, S. Holly, with others. *Protecting Children from Abuse and Neglect: Developing and Maintaining Effective Support Systems for Families.* San Francisco, CA: Jossey-Bass Publishers, 1980.

Gibelman, Margaret, and Grant, Stuart. "The Uses and Misuses of Central Registries in Child Protective Services." *Child Welfare* LVII, 1 (July–August 1978): 405–413.

Gil, David G., ed. *Child Abuse and Violence.* New York: AMS Press, Inc., 1979.

———. *Violence Against Children—Physical Child Abuse in the United States.* Cambridge, MA: Harvard University Press, 1970.

Giovannoni, Jeanne M., and Becerra, Rosina M. *Defining Child Abuse.* New York: The Free Press, 1979.

Gleeson, James P. "Implementing Structured Decision-Making Procedures at Child Welfare Intake." *Child Welfare* LXVI, 2 (March–April 1987): 101–112.

Goldstein, Joseph; Freud, Anna; and Solnit, Albert J. *Before the Best Interests of the Child.* New York: The Free Press, 1979.

Gothard, Sol. "The Admissibility of Evidence in Child Sexual Abuse Cases." *Child Welfare* LXVI, 1 (January–February 1987): 13–24.

Harris, Janice C., and Bernstein, Barton E. "Lawyer and Social Worker as a Team: Preparing for Trial in Neglect Cases." *Child Welfare* LIX, 8 (September–October 1980): 469–477.

Helfer, Ray E., and Kempe, Ruth S., eds. *The Battered Child.* 4th ed. Chicago: University of Chicago Press, 1987.

Holder, Wayne, and Hayes, Kathleen, eds. *Malpractice and Liability in Child Protective Services.* Longmont, CO: Bookmakers Guild, 1984.

———, and Mohr, Cynthia, eds. *Helping in Child Protective Services.* Englewood, CO: American Humane Association, 1980.

Jones, Mary Ann, and Botsko, Michael. *Parental Lack of Supervision—Nature and Consequences of a Major Child Neglect Problem.* Washington, DC: Child Welfare League of America, 1987.

Jones, Mary Ann; Magura, Stephen; and Shyne, Ann W. "Effective Practice with Families in Protective and Preventive Services: What Works?" *Child Welfare* LX, 2 (February 1981): 67–80.

Johnson, Barbara Brooks. "Sexual Abuse and Prevention: A Rural Interdisciplinary Effort." *Child Welfare* LXVI, 2 (March–April 1987): 165–173.

Junewicz, Walter J. "A Protective Posture Toward Emotional Neglect and Abuse." *Child Welfare* LXII, 3 (May–June 1983): 243–252.

Kadushin, Alfred, and Martin, Judith A. *Child Abuse—An Interactional Event*. New York: Columbia University Press, 1981.

Kelleher, Maureen E. "Investigating Institutional Abuse: A Post-Substantiation Model." *Child Welfare* LXVI, 4 (July–August 1987): 343–351.

Kempe, C. Henry, and Helfer, Ray E. *Helping the Battered Child and His Family*. Philadelphia, PA: J.B. Lippincott Company, 1972.

Kroth, Jerome A. *Child Sexual Abuse: Analysis of a Family Therapy Approach*. Springfield, IL: Charles C. Thomas, 1979.

MacFarlane, Kee, and Waterman, Jill, with Conerly, Shawn, Damon, Linda, Durfee, Michael, and Long, Suzanne. *Sexual Abuse of Young Children*. New York: The Guilford Press, 1986.

Magura, Stephen, and Moses, Beth. "Clients as Evaluators in Child Protective Services." *Child Welfare* LXVIII, 2 (March–April 1984): 99–112.

———, and ———. *Outcome Measures for Child Welfare Services: Child Well-Being Scales and Rating Forms*. Washington, DC: Child Welfare League of America, 1987.

———; ———; and Jones, Mary Ann. *Assessing Risk and Measuring Change in Families: The Family Risk Scales*. Washington, DC: Child Welfare League of America, 1987.

Martin, Harold P., ed. *The Abused Child: A Multidisciplinary Approach to Developmental Issues and Treatment*. Cambridge, MA: Ballinger Publishing Co., 1976.

Meddin, Barbara J. "Criteria for Placement Decisions in Protective Services." *Child Welfare* LXIII, 4 (July–August 1984): 367–373.

Morgan, Sharon R. *Abuse and Neglect of Handicapped Children*. Boston: Little, Brown and Company, 1987.

Mouzakitis, Chris Michael, and Goldstein, Susan C. "A Multidisciplinary Approach to Treating Child Neglect." *Social Casework* 66, 4 (April 1985): 218–224.

Nelson, Gordon K.; Dainauski, Jane; and Kilmer, Lori. "Child Abuse Reporting Laws: Action and Uncertainty." *Child Welfare* LIX, 4 (April 1980): 203–212.

Polansky, Norman A. "There is Nothing So Practical as a Good Theory." *Child Welfare* LXV, 1 (January–February 1986): 3–15.

———. *Treating Loneliness in Child Protection*. Washington, DC: Child Welfare League of America, 1986.

———; DeSoix, Christine; and Sharlin, Shlomo A. *Understanding and Reaching the Parent*. New York: Child Welfare League of America, 1972.

———, et al. *Damaged Parents: An Anatomy of Child Neglect*. Chicago: University of Chicago Press, 1981.

Rindfleisch, Nolan, and Hicho, Donna. "Institutional Child Protection: Issues in Program Development and Implementation." *Child Welfare* LXVI, 4 (July–August 1987): 329–342.

———, and Rabb, Joel. "Dilemmas in Planning for the Protection of Children and Youths in Residential Facilities." *Child Welfare* LXIII, 3 (May–June 1984): 205–215.

Rosick, Don C. "A Model for Systematic Child Protective Service Training." *Child Welfare* LVIII, 7 (July–August 1979): 429–433.

Sgroi, Suzanne M. *Vulnerable Populations: Evaluation and Treatment of Sexually Abused Children and Adult Survivors*. Volume I. Lexington, MA: D.C. Heath and Company, 1988.

Shapiro, Deborah. *Parents and Protectors: A Study in Child Abuse and Neglect*. New York: Research Center, Child Welfare League of America, 1979.

Stein, Theodore J. "The Child Abuse Prevention and Treatment Act." *Social Service Review* 58, 2 (June 1984): 302–314.

Stuart, Irving R., and Greer, Joanne G., eds. *Victims of Sexual Aggression: Treatment of Children, Women, and Men*. New York: Van Nostrand Reinhold Company, 1984.

Urban Systems Research and Engineering, Inc. *A Survey of Substantiated Cases of Child Abuse by Mothers in Child Protective Services to Determine the Mother's Age at the Time of Her First Child's Birth.* Washington, DC: National Center for Child Abuse and Neglect, ACYF, 1988. Mimeo.

U.S. Department of Health, Education, and Welfare. *Protective Services for Abused and Neglected Children and Their Families. A Guide for State and Local Departments of Public Social Services on the Delivery of Protective Services.* Washington, DC: USDHEW, Social and Rehabilitation Service, Public Services Administration, 1977.

Wald, Michael S. *State Intervention on Behalf of "Neglected" Children: Standards for Removal of Children from Their Homes, Monitoring the Status of Children in Foster Care, and Termination of Parental Rights.* Stanford, CA: Stanford University Press, 1976.

———; Carlsmith, J.M.; and Leiderman, P.H. *Protecting Abused and Neglected Children.* Stanford, CA: Stanford University Press, 1988.

Wasserman, Saul, and Rosenfeld, Alvin. "Decision-making in Child Abuse and Neglect." *Child Welfare* LXV, 6 (November–December 1986): 515–529.

Whiteman, Martin; Fanshel, David; and Grundy, John F. "Cognitive-Behavioral Interventions Aimed at Anger of Parents at Risk of Child Abuse." *Social Work* 32, 6 (November–December 1987): 469–474.

Whiting, Leila. "Defining Emotional Neglect." *Children Today* 5, 1 (January–February 1976): 2–5.

Williams, Gertrude J., and Money, John, eds. *Traumatic Abuse and Neglect of Children at Home.* Baltimore, MD: Johns Hopkins University Press, 1980.

INDEX

A

Abuse: child, in nonfamilial situations, 0.4; child sexual, 0.2, 1.1; emotional, 0.3; in child caring facility, 5.7; physical, 1.1; preventing child, outside the family, 5.4; receiving reports of, 1.8; response to intrafamilial cases of, 0.7; response to nonfamilial cases of, 0.8

Accountability, agency, 4.14-4.21; public, 4.20

Accuracy of case records, 4.8

Administration, organization and, 4.1-4.28

Administrators, qualifications and responsibilities of, 4.23

Advisory board, responsibilities of, 4.4

Advocacy in behalf of vulnerable children and families, 6.3

Agencies: attorney for, 3.6; referral from other, 1.5; relationships with other, 4.21; work with other, 1.5

Agency: budget, 4.18; manual, 4.5; operations, evaluation of, 4.17; organization and administration of, 4.1-4.28; program evaluation, 4.16; responsibilities and duties of, 1.4; role of, 6.4; role of licensing, 6.11

Anonymous reports, 1.6

Appeal, right to, 4.13

Assess risk, sources of information to, 1.11

Assessment: of reports, 1.8-1.13; of risk to the child, 1.10; results of, 1.13

Attorney, use of, 3.6

Auspices, public agency, 4.2

Authority: of the social worker in protective service, 2.2; 2.5; to remove a child from own home, 1.18; to remove the offender, 1.15

Authorization, 4.1

Availability of service, 1.14, 1.17

B

Basic principles, 0.5

Board of directors, see governing boards

Budget, agency, 4.19

Business, role of, 6.9

C

Career ladder work environment, 4.27

Caseloads, 4.28

Case planning, 2.4

Case records, 4.8; accuracy in, 4.8; confidentiality of, 1.12, 4.8, 4.12

Casework, 2.3

Central registry (see service information system)

Characteristics, of child protective services, 1.3

Child protection, recent developments in, 0.2, 0.3

Child: assessment of risk to, 1.10; emergency services for, 1.17; fatalities, review of, 4.18; for whom service is appropriate, 1.1; hospitalized, 2.6; legal representation for, 3.8; placement of, 3.8; rights of, 0.6; removal of, 1.18; social work with, 2.6; work with, regarding court proceedings, 3.10

Children: emergency shelter services for, 1.17; role of the court in the protection of, 3.1-3.14; testimony of, 3.8; vulnerable, advocacy in behalf of, 6.3

Child welfare service, protective service as a specialized practice, 1.3, 2.1, 2.7, 2.8, 4.7

Citizens, private, reports from, 1.6

Community: networks, role of, 6.2; relations, 4.21; reports of abuse and neglect, 1.5; responsibility for protecting children, 6.1-6.12

Community organization, 2.3

Compensation, of victim, 3.14

Complaints (see reporting of neglect and/or abuse)

Compliance with state or provincial child abuse and neglect reporting laws, 5.2

Confidentiality: 4.12; agency policy on, 1.12; of case records, 4.8; public guidelines for, 4.12; safeguards regarding, 4.10

Considerations, special practice, 2.7, 2.8

Consultants: medical, 2.9; mental health, 2.10; use of, 2.9, 2.10

Cooperation with courts, 3.1-3.14; with law enforcement officials, 2.7

Corporal punishment, 5.1

Court: role of, in protecting children, 3.1-3.14

Court action, helping parents understand, 3.9; initiating, 3.2

Credentialing authorities, role of, 6.12

Criminal court, use of, in protecting children, 3.4

Criminal records, screening individuals and agencies with past, 5.10; screening potential licensees and employees, 5.9

Crises counseling, group and individual, 1.14

Cultural differences, 1.10, 1.17, 2.6

D

Data from central registry, safeguards on use of, 4.10

Day care services, 1.14

Death of child (see fatalities)

Decision making, 1.10, 1.13

Definition, of abuse or neglect of child, 1.1; of protective service, 1.1-1.3, 2.1, 4.5

Developmental, staff, 4.26, 5.13

Developments, recent, in child protection, 0.2, 0.3

Differential use of personnel, 2.8

Director of protective services, 4.23

Directors, board of (see governing boards)

Direct social work with child, 2.6; with parents, 2.5

Distinctive characteristics of child protective service, 1.3

Domestic relations court, use of, in protecting children, 3.5

Duration of child protective service, 1.19

Duties and responsibilities, of agency, 1.4

E

Educational services, 1.14

Emergency financial services, 1.14

Emergency shelter services for children, 1.17

Emotional: abuse, 0.3; maltreatment, 1.1

Employees, preemployment checks of, 5.9

Ethnic considerations, 1.10, 1.17, 2.6

Evaluation: in case records, 4.8; of agency operations, 4.17; of agency program, 4.16

Expert testimony, use of, 3.7

Expungement of information from reports, 4.11

F

Factors to be considered with regard to short-term out-of-home services, 1.16

Families: for whom service is appropriate, 1.1; vulnerable, advocacy in behalf of, 6.3

Family: in-home support services for, 1.14; protecting children placed away from, 5.1-5.14; rights and responsibilities of, 0.6

Family court: initiation of action by, 3.2; role of, 3.1; use of, in protecting chil-

dren, 3.3
Family planning, 1.14
Family therapy, 2.3
Fatalities, review of child, 4.18
Financing, 4.7, 4.19
Frame of reference for protective service, 0.5-0.8

G

Generic or specialized approach to providing protective service, 4.28
Governing boards, responsibilities of, 4.3; role of, 6.5
Governmental facilities, protecting children in, 5.6
Groupwork, 2.3

H

Health care, 6.6; services, 1.14
Helping parents understand court action, 3.9
Historical highlights, 0.1
Home, removal of the child from, 1.18
Housing services, 1.14

I

Inappropriate reports, 1.7
Information: a centralized system of, 4.9-4.13; on case activity, 4.8; reliability of, 4.8; sources of, to assess risk, 1.11; to parents about rights relating to court, 3.9; to support allegations to the court, 3.2
In-home support services for family stabilization, 0.7; 1.14
Initiation of juvenile and family court action, 3.2
Intake workers, number of cases, 4.28
Intrafamilial cases of child abuse and neglect, response to, 0.7
Investigation (see Intake)

J

Juvenile court: initiation of action by, 3.2; role of, 3.1; use of, in protecting children, 3.3

L

Language differences, 1.17, 2.6, 3.9, 3.13, 4.14
Law enforcement and child protective services, 2.7
Laws, reporting, compliance with, 5.2
Legal services, 1.14; use of, 3.6
Licensees, potential, prelicensure checks of, 5.9
Licensing agency, role of, 6.11
Licensing responsibilities of state or provincial and local agencies, 5.8

M

Manual, agency, 4.5
Media, role of, 6.10
Medical: consultant, 2.9; practitioners, role of, 6.6; services, 1.14
Mental health: consultant, 2.10; practitioners, role of 6.6; services, 1.14
Methods, social work, 2.3
Monitoring, of agency program, 5.14
Multidisciplinary team, 1.9

N

Neglect: in families for whom service is appropriate, 1.1; in nonfamilial situations, 0.4; preventing child, outside the family, 5.4; receiving reports of, 1.8; response to intrafamilial cases of, 0.7; response to nonfamilial cases of, 0.8
Nonemployed adults present in the child care setting, 5.12
Nonfamilial: cases of child abuse and neglect, response to, 0.8; child abuse and neglect, 0.4; role of protective service in, 5.3
Number of families for a full-time practitioner, 4.28
Number of investigation/intake cases, 4.28
Number of supervisors, 4.28

O

Offender, removal of the, 1.15
Ongoing cases, number of, 4.28

ing, of abuse and neglect, 1.8

Research, 4.15

Respite care, 1.14

Response: to intrafamilial cases of child abuse and neglect, 0.7; to nonfamilial cases of child abuse and neglect, 0.8; to report, 1.9

Responsibilities: agency, 1.4; licensing, 5.8; of administrators, 4.23; of advisory boards, 4.4; of board of directors, 4.3; of social workers, 4.25; of supervisors, 4.24; parental, 0.6

Results of assessment, 1.13

Review of child fatalities, 4.18

Right to appeal, 4.13

Rights and responsibilities within the family, 0.6

Risk: sources of information to assess, 1.11; to the child, assessment of, 1.10

Role of: agency, 6.4; board of directors, 6.5; business, 6.9; child protective service in protecting children outside the family, 5.3; community networks, 6.2; credentialing authorities, 6.12; juvenile or family court, 3.1; licensing agency, 6.11; mental health and medical care practitioners, 6.6; parents, 6.1; public schools, 6.7; social and religious organizations, 6.8; the court in protecting children, 3.1-3.14; the media, 6.10

S

Safeguards on use of data from central registry, 4.10

School facilities, public, protecting children in, 5.5; role of, 6.7

Selection of personnel, 4.22

Services: duration of, 1.19; emergency shelter, 1.17; in-home support, 1.14; legal, 3.6; short-term out-of-home, 1.16; termination of, 1.20

Services: purchase of, 4.7; specialized, 4.6

Service information system, 4.9-4.13 (Central Registry)

Serving as a witness, 3.12

Sexual abuse: child, 0.2, 1.1

Shelter services, emergency, 1.17

Short-term out-of-home services, factors to

be considered with regard to , 1.16

Siblings; placement of, 1.16, 1.18, 2.6, 3.3

Social organizations, role of, 6.8

Social work: in child protective services, 2.1-2.10; methods, 2.3; personnel, 4.22-4.28; with child, 2.6; with parents, 2.5

Social worker: authority of, in child protective service, 2.2; qualifications and responsibilities of, 4.25

Sources of information to assess risk, 1.11

Special practice considerations, 2.7-2.8

Specialized or generic approach to providing protective service, 4.28

Specialized: practice, child protective service as a, 2.1; service, 4.6

Stabilization of family, support services for, 1.14

Staff training, 4.26, 5.13

State or provincial: licensing responsibilities, 5.8; reporting laws, compliance with, 5.2

Statistics, use of, 4.14

Substance abuse services, 1.14

Substantiated reports, 1.13

Supervisors: number of, 4.28; qualifications and responsibilities of, 4.24

Support services, in-home, 1.14

Supportive personnel, 2.8

T

Teamwork, 1.9

Termination of child protective service, 1.20

Testimony: of children and parents, 3.8; use of expert, 3.7

Training, of staff, 4.26; 5.13

U

Unsubstantiated reports, 1.13

Use of: authority, 2.2; consultants, 2.9, 2.10; criminal court in protecting children, 3.4; domestic relations court in protecting children, 3.5; expert testimony, 3.7; juvenile or family court in protecting children, 3.3; legal services, 3.6; statistics, 4.14

V

W